The Fruits of Fatima

Joseph Pronechen

The Fruits
of Fatima

A Century of
Signs and Wonders

SOPHIA INSTITUTE PRESS

Manchester, New Hampshire

Sophia Institute Press
Box 5284, Manchester, NH 03108
1-800-888-9344

www.SophiaInstitute.com

Sophia Institute Press® is a registered trademark of Sophia Institute.

Library of Congress Cataloging-in-Publication Data

Names: Pronechen, Joseph, author.
Title: The fruits of Fatima : a century of signs and wonders / Joseph Pronechen.
Description: Manchester, New Hampshire : Sophia Institute Press, [2019] | Includes bibliographical references. | Summary: "The author looks at various aspects and lesser-known incidents related to the apparitions at Fatima and explains how they can help us live out the message of Fatima"—Provided by publisher.
Identifiers: LCCN 2019022862 | ISBN 9781622828142 (paperback)
Subjects: LCSH: Mary, Blessed Virgin, Saint—Apparitions and miracles—Portugal—Fátima. | Mary, Blessed Virgin, Saint—Prayers and devotions. | Fatima, Our Lady of—History.
Classification: LCC BT660.F3 P76 2019 | DDC 232.91/70946945—dc23
LC record available at https://lccn.loc.gov/2019022862

First printing

For the three most important women in my life:

Our Blessed Mother, Mary, who has always been at my side with her motherly concern and ever-present help;

My wife, Mary, who is by far the best loving helpmate a husband could have, a tower of constant love, and the model woman described in Sirach 26:1–4, 13–18;

My mother, Pauline, who sacrificed much and was a constant example of prayer and trusting in Jesus.

Contents

The Fruits of Fatima

Introduction

The Miracle of the Sun, which took place in Fatima on October 13, 1917, is likely the greatest miracle since the ones recorded in the New Testament.

Between the occurrences in the New Testament and those at Fatima, there have been other miracles of magnificent scale. One that immediately comes to mind happened at the Battle of Lepanto on October 7, 1571. The victory of the greatly outnumbered ragtag Holy League naval force, hastily formed by Pope St. Pius V to defend against a massive invasion of ships heading toward Europe, was immediately attributed to Our Lady and the Rosary. The result was that October 7 was declared the feast of Our Lady of Victory, soon to be renamed the feast of Our Lady of the Rosary.

But then came October 13, 1917, and the Miracle of the Sun. Thanks be to God, it startled more than seventy thousand people who were witnesses at the Cova da Iria that day. Many had come as pilgrims, others as scoffers. Many of the pilgrims had their faith strengthened. As for the scoffers, a number of them became believers. Even the secular newspaper reporters who came with a jaundiced eye, surely ready to prove the young seers to be frauds, reported in amazement what took place.

The Fruits of Fatima

It was the miracle that Our Lady of Fatima had promised in July, when she told the children, "In October I will tell you who I am and what I want. I will then perform a miracle so that all may believe." In August, she repeated, "In the last month I will perform a miracle so that all may believe." Again, in September she reminded them, "In October I will perform a miracle so that all may believe."

Our Blessed Mother had appeared every month, beginning in May 1917, and that October 13, during her final appearance, she performed the miracle she had spoken of. She also identified herself as Our Lady of the Rosary, repeating what she told the children during each apparition: pray the Rosary daily for peace — a message she meant for every single person.

Along with the Miracle of the Sun, there are many fascinating, surprising, and little-known facts connected with the Fatima apparitions. The extraordinary events, which continued for years after the apparitions, further reveal and support the messages Our Lady conveyed not only to the children but to every one of us.

These surprising, forgotten, or little-known facts, from the obscure to the significant, will help us to understand the Fatima apparitions better, to see how others were affected by them, and to weave together amazing providential occurrences, adding more layers of meaning and proof of heaven's plan — and maybe even give us a chuckle or two.

If we are Mary's children — and we *are* — then it's time to learn more about Fatima. May the little-known facts and incidents in these pages give us new insights into Fatima and help us to discover and respond to the requests of our Mother.

1

Fatima's Wonders and Post-Apparition Phenomena

Let's begin with the biggest wonder of all — the Miracle of the Sun, which was foretold by our Blessed Mother. The phenomenon not only reached the seventy thousand people at the Cova, but it has also reached across the decades to all of us. Father Ignacio Lorenco was, at the time, a nine-year-old in a village eleven miles away. He described how the village children were outside and witnessed "the great Miracle, which one could see quite distinctly from the top of the hill where my village was situated." The sun, he said, "suddenly seemed to come down in a zigzag, menacing the earth. Terrified, I ran and hid myself among the people, who were weeping and expecting the end of the world at any moment."

Many nonbelievers converted that day. Father Lorenco noted, "Near us was an unbeliever who had spent the morning mocking the simpletons who had gone off to Fatima just to see an ordinary girl. He now seemed to be paralyzed, his eyes fixed on the sun. Afterwards he trembled from head to foot and, lifting up his arms, fell on his knees in the mud, crying out to Our Lady."[1]

[1] "100 Years of Fatima," EWTN, www.ewtn.com/fatima/sixth-apparition-of-our-lady.asp.

The Fruits of Fatima

Father Lorenco said that people were asking God to forgive their sins. "We all ran to the two chapels in the village, which were soon filled to the point of overflowing. During those long moments of the solar prodigy, objects around us turned all the colors of the rainbow. We saw ourselves blue, yellow, red, etc.... When the people realized that the danger was over, there was an explosion of joy, and everyone joined in thanksgiving and praise to Our Lady."[2]

Of course, most of the observers were at the scene—armies of eyewitnesses at the Cova da Iria, tens of thousands of them, fourteen times the population of the city of Leiria (which would be reestablished as a diocese three months later). Let's take a quick look at a few descriptions that set the scene.

Jacinta and Francisco's father, Ti Marto, said it was most extraordinary that the sun didn't hurt their eyes. "Everything was still and quiet, and everyone was looking up. Then at a certain moment, the sun appeared to stop spinning. It then began to move and to dance in the sky until it seemed to detach itself from its place and fall upon us. It was a terrible moment."[3]

Maria de Capelinha, who later became custodian of the original chapel built at the site, described how everything turned "different colors—yellow, blue, and white." Then the sun "shook and trembled." She said, "It looked like a wheel of fire that was going to fall on the people. They began to cry out, 'We shall all be killed!' Others called to Our Lady to save

---

[2] Ibid.

[3] Father John de Marchi, I.M.C, *The True Story of Fatima* (St. Paul, MN: Catechetical Guild Educational Society, 1952), www. ewtn.com/library/MARY/TSFATIMA.htm, chap. "Our Lady Appears."

them. They recited acts of contrition. One woman began to confess her sins aloud.... When at last the sun stopped leaping and moving, we all breathed a sigh of relief. We were still alive, and the miracle, which the children had foretold, had been seen by everyone."[4]

Dr. Almeida Garret, a professor from Coimbra University, described the vision in vivid detail, from the sun looking like "a glazed wheel made of mother-of-pearl," to noting that it "spun round on itself in a mad whirl. Then, suddenly, one heard a clamor, a cry of anguish breaking from all the people. The sun, whirling wildly, seemed to loosen itself from the firmament and advance threateningly upon the earth, as if to crush us with its huge and fiery weight. The sensation during those moments was terrible."[5]

Looking at the horizon, Garret reported seeing everything and everybody appearing the color of amethyst.[6]

He also said, "Fearing impairment of the retina, which was improbable because then I would not have seen everything in purple," he turned around and, with his back to what he had witnessed, opened his eyes and saw "that the landscape and the air retained the purple hue."[7]

As the moments went on, he "heard a peasant nearby say, 'This lady looks yellow.' As a matter of fact, everything far and near had changed now. People seemed to have jaundice." He looked at his hands, and they, too, looked yellow.[8]

---

[4]   Ibid.

[5]   Ibid.

[6]   Ibid.

[7]   John Haffert, *Russia Will Be Converted*, vol. 1 (Washington, NJ: AMI International Press, 1950), 52.

[8]   Ibid.

More than the color change was the change in so many hearts, something even the somewhat anticlerical Lisbon newspaper couldn't help but report. It described the event with respect, even awe at times, mentioning how the spectators were shouting, "A miracle! A miracle!" The account also recalled the reverence of an elderly man: "With his face turned to the sun, he recited the Credo in a loud voice.... I saw him afterwards going up to those around him who still had their hats on and vehemently imploring them to uncover before such an extraordinary demonstration of the existence of God."[9]

Then, after the Miracle of the Sun, there followed right away another phenomenon. When people had arrived at the Cova, they were drenched by the pouring rain that had gone on for hours. The ground was a sea of mud. Yet, once the miracle ended and the sun resumed its normal place in the sky, everybody's clothes were perfectly dry, and the mud was no more. Heaven had taken care of everything. Like a good mother who wants her children dry on a rainy day, Our Lady surely had a hand in seeing that all her children were provided for.

Other phenomena added to the intense spiritual atmosphere. It's as if these added wonders were also witnesses to and echoes of heaven's visit. Let's take a look at one of these echoes, which one eyewitness and others near the three children of Fatima—Lucia, Jacinta, and Francisco—saw on that October 13.

We have to stop for a moment, however, to consider the Church's position on miracles. The Miracle of the Sun has always been called a miracle by those in the Church and even by a pope who saw the phenomenon (we'll get to that Holy Father later). All the healings and other wonders witnessed at Fatima, we'll

---

[9] De Marchi, *True Story*, 103.

call wonders and phenomena. Or we'll use the word "miracle" in its common sense, for something that is naturally unexplainable.

The reason for this distinction concerns the Church's extremely strict (and what have today been called nearly impossible) conditions for official recognition of an approved supernatural miracle. Apart from the causes for canonization, there isn't time for the long examinations and complex procedures conducted by a board of specialists who examine every fine detail of the case under the proverbial microscope before declaring something a miracle. They look for any and every natural explanation first.[10]

So, unless something thought to be miraculous goes through rigorous testing, the Church cannot and does not call it an official miracle. Otherwise, the word "miracle" is used in the common sense. Other than the truly miraculous Miracle of the Sun — because the apparitions at Fatima were approved by popes — we'll refer to all the other extraordinary incidents and signs connected with Fatima simply as wonders and phenomena.

Let's get to the wonders and phenomena.

In the late 1990s, a man named Carl Malburg had the privilege of speaking with a woman who was present at the Miracle of the Sun. He wanted to ask her about it, but she really wanted to tell him about the little-known second wonder that happened shortly after she and the rest of the onlookers saw the sun dancing in the sky, hurling toward earth, then returning to its place in the heavens.

[10] On another note, the Vatican's *Norms regarding the Manner of Proceeding in the Discernment of Presumed Apparitions or Revelations*, approved by Pope Paul VI, states that in the case of apparitions, "the duty of vigilance and intervention falls to the Ordinary of the place" — the local bishop.

The Fruits of Fatima

Malburg met this woman in his travels. At the time of this interview,[11] he was working with John Haffert, who, decades earlier, had cofounded the Blue Army, officially known as the World Apostolate of Fatima. Haffert had an early Pilgrim Virgin statue from Portugal that had been blessed by the Fatima bishop and was eventually given by his widow to the Blue Army.

Throughout the years Malburg traveled with Haffert, he had encountered several people who were distant relatives of one of the Fatima families. He said that one of them "told me their aunt or uncle had a cure there." But this woman was the first he had met who was there on that day of the Miracle of the Sun—and saw something else too.

In 1997, while traveling through parishes, hospitals, and nursing homes with the Pilgrim Virgin statue, Malburg found himself in San Diego. There, a woman told him that her mother had witnessed the Miracle of the Sun. The woman told him, "My mother has always wished to be interviewed because she's always wanted to tell the story. She is still living, ninety-two years old now. She insists Our Lady is keeping her mind sharp until someone interviews her."

Malburg told this woman that he didn't know Portuguese but would get someone else to translate. He chuckled as the woman answered, "My mother's lived in America since 1942. She lost all her Portuguese years ago."

Since this was the first witness of the Miracle of the Sun whom Malburg had encountered, he asked Haffert to go with him to talk to her. But Haffert told him to go by himself.

---

[11] Personal interview with Malburg, April 2017; see also Joseph Pronechen, "Fatima's Other Miracle after the Sun Danced," *National Catholic Register*, May 9, 2017, www.ncregister.com/blog/joseph-pronechen/fatimas-other-miracle-after-the-sun-danced.

"I found out why she thought she should be interviewed," he remarked after seeing the woman. "She said she was twelve and that she and the other girls — four of them — walked all the way up from the coast to Fatima."

Malburg continued with the story as the elderly woman told it:

> We were children, and we pushed our way through the crowd. We came really close to the center where the apparitions would be, and we climbed on some rocks and blocked the view of people behind. We could look down and see [everything]. The three children [Lucia, Jacinta, and Francisco] would never have gotten there unless carried on the shoulders of some big men who pushed their way through the crowds.

Malburg didn't go into detail about what the woman, whose name has disappeared from the annals of time, said about the sun, but he said, "She wanted to tell me something else. She moved on because there was another miracle not in the books."

She told him that "a lot of people picked the twigs and leaves of the bushes to take" because they smelled so good, so aromatic. Those went quickly. "But we picked up some pebbles around the bush [by where Our Lady appeared] because they would smell good too," she explained. Malburg was amazed to find that, eighty years later, she still had those pebbles in her dresser drawer, making her clothes smell fresh even then.

The woman continued her story, saying, "People put their rosaries on the ground. They knew what way the Blessed Mother would face, and they put their rosaries out there in front of the place. [The pile of] rosaries was shaped like a cross."

And after the apparition?

The Fruits of Fatima

The woman explained, "There were so many that when everybody went to get their rosaries back, they were all tangled up. And everyone was trying to find the right rosary."

"The men had the three children up on their shoulders again," she said. Malburg interjected, "Otherwise they would be buffeted and smothered—I knew that for a fact." The woman also told him about the girls' new dresses and people pulling off pieces of the lace to keep. Malburg knew about that, too.

"It was all adding up except the rosaries," he said. Then she continued, "One of the children saw that the people's rosaries were all tangled. Then the children slid down from the shoulders, took a handful of [the tangled] rosaries, and simply passed them out—none were tangled! And everybody got the right rosary! We watched that happen!" she told Malburg, still amazed, after so many decades, at that second spiritual marvel.

The woman had waited most of her lifetime for someone to come along and interview her about what she and her friends had witnessed—the pile of rosaries miraculously untangled, and each one returned to its proper owner without the three visionaries knowing who in that crowd owned which one.

"My wife and I got goosebumps listening to that," Malburg recalled.

He then asked Haffert, "Are you aware that people laid their rosaries in the mud hoping to get a blessing on them?" No one had ever told him that, he answered.

"This lady told me that a lot of rosaries were laid around the bush," Malburg said, and he repeated the woman's story to Haffert.

Haffert answered, "Why would you doubt it?"

About ten years later, Malburg came across a magazine article in Portugal that verified this event. "This truly was one of the highlights," he said, marveling again at the story of this little-known phenomenon at Fatima that happened right after the sun danced in the sky.

These kinds of events did not take place only after the last of the apparitions of Our Lady of Fatima; rather, they began much earlier, during the stretch of months from the first to the final apparition. Heaven was giving substantial hints through extraordinary happenings that these were, indeed, true apparitions despite the scoffers. And they weren't for the three shepherd children only. While the Fatima children — Lucia and her cousins Jacinta and Francisco — saw the Blessed Mother at each apparition, some people who came to the Cova da Iria on those days also experienced supernatural "extras."

One took place at the apparition on September 13. This apparition ended with an astonishing phenomenon that is rarely mentioned, although it was surely a spectacular heavenly sign and a tiny preview of that yet unknown but promised miracle of October.

In his book *Fatima: Cove of Wonders*, Father Alphonse Cappa, S.S.P., gives a splendid description of this event, deserving of being fully quoted:

> There occurred a most singular phenomenon, never before witnessed by the assembled people in the Cova.
>
> From the pale but cloudless sky there came a shower of white petals, resembling snowflakes but melting before they touched the ground or the bodies of the astounded people.
>
> Later on, in various pilgrimages, and on the anniversary of the first apparition of the Virgin, this phenomenon was repeated, as attested to and confirmed by reliable witnesses, including the bishop of the diocese to which Fatima belongs.

Furthermore, as proof of the incontrovertible evidence, on May 13, 1924, Antonio Rebelo Martins, vice-consul in the United States, produced a photographic plate of the supernatural prodigy, verified by legal testimony.[12]

As Our Lady appeared, heaven smiled and got people to look up and ready themselves for the great miracle to come in two months' time. But that was not the only phenomenon people witnessed that September 13. More heavenly surprises were visible to many gathered there.

At the holm oak tree, the three shepherd children knelt as usual and started praying the Rosary. All those gathered at the site had also knelt to pray along with them when Lucia, Jacinta, and Francisco saw the flash of light that announced Our Lady.

Then came a surprise for the pilgrims. Again, in Cappa's well-researched book (its primary sources including a priest who worked directly with the bishop of Leiria as well as Sister Lucia herself, who had the final review of his manuscript), he describes what the people saw:

> The sun suddenly lost its splendor. The hue of the surrounding atmosphere changed to a yellowish gold. Then a delightful cry went up from the multitude: 'She comes! Look! There!! There! How beautiful!'
>
> A small, luminous, global cloud was recognized immediately as the footstool of the invisible Lady. It moved in from the East toward the West slowly and majestically. Slowly it descended to rest, hovering above the holm oak, the tree of wonders.

[12] Fr. Alphonse Cappa, S.S.P., *Fatima: Cove of Wonders* (Boston, MA: St. Paul Editions, 1979), 78.

Something similar happened on August 13 when the children were carried off to jail, while up to eighteen thousand people waited for them at the Cova. Learning that the children were imprisoned, the crowd grew angry but was quickly calmed by heaven itself.

Many who were there described hearing what they thought was an explosion or thunder coming from the cloudless blue sky, and after it, seeing a flash of brilliant light. Then they said that the "sun paled," the atmosphere turned "a yellowish gold, and a small cloud, most beautiful in its ethereal form, came and hovered over the forlorn-looking holm oak." The crowd shouted, "Look! Look! It is a sign from Our Lady!"[13]

Now, on September 13, they again saw this phenomenon when the "kneeling, ecstatic figures of the children were transfigured in a light that seemed to change the spot into a Holy of Holies, filled with the majesty of God."[14]

Of course, only the three children saw Our Lady.

A witness that day, identified as S. Bento in his testimony (which is included in a book of documents and letters on Fatima)[15] wrote that on September 13 the people became excited as they described what they saw in the sky: "Some said they were stars, others that they saw a dove, and yet others that they saw shooting. There was great excitement! There were still others who said that everyone saw flowers falling from the sky."

---

[13] Ibid., 68–69.

[14] Ibid., 76–77.

[15] See Fr. Antonio Maria Martins, S.J., ed., *Documents on Fatima and Memoirs of Sister Lucia* (Waite Park, MN: Fatima Family Apostolate, 2002), chap. 14.

Mr. Bento also reported on what happened during the July 13 apparition at the Cova. He said there was a wisp of smoke at the time of the apparition. (Could it have been a visible sign of the cloud under Our Lady's feet?)

He went on to say that the sun, which had been beating down quite "fiercely," as it was summertime, suddenly stopped giving off heat. He also explained, "Many people said that they heard the Apparition when it spoke but that they could not make out what it was saying. I only heard when Lucia said, 'There she goes.' I heard a rumble in the air that sounded like the beginning of thunder."

To capture peoples' attention and turn their minds and hearts to the apparitions of Our Lady and to prepare them for the great Miracle of the Sun, these heavenly signs were manifested to the pilgrim crowds.

The three child visionaries began to face hostility from local authorities, and on August 13, they were put in jail, preventing them from being at the Cova for that month's apparition. Although the anti-religious civil authorities might have delayed Our Lady's appearance to the children, however, they couldn't cancel it. The children heroically survived their imprisonment, and Our Lady appeared to them two days later, after they had been brought home. That afternoon, Lucia and Francisco and his brother Joao were grazing the sheep at Valinhos, near where the Angel of Peace had appeared to them twice in 1916. Lucia wrote that they felt something "supernatural approaching and enveloping" them. She went on to say:

> Suspecting that Our Lady was about to appear to us, and feeling sorry lest Jacinta might miss seeing her, we asked her brother to go and call her.

Meanwhile, Francisco and I saw the flash of light, which we called lightning. Jacinta arrived, and a moment later, we saw Our Lady on a holm oak tree.[16]

When Our Lady left, and the apparition ended, the children broke off the branches of the holm oak tree on which she had placed her feet.

When an overjoyed Jacinta told her aunt that they had seen Our Lady again, her aunt accused her of lying. But Our Lady came to the rescue. Unshaken, Jacinta showed her aunt the branches and pointed out, "She had one foot here and one here."[17]

When the skeptical aunt looked at them, Lucia wrote, "She was surprised by the wonderful scent the branches exuded. She did not know what to say."[18]

A heavenly fragrance has at times accompanied a miracle or the apparition of a saint. The Church calls it "the odor of sanctity." This time, the beautiful fragrance made a believer of the aunt.

But the story didn't end there. That day, the branches from the holm oak suddenly disappeared. No one knew what became of them.

Decades later, not long before Jacinta and Francisco were beatified, their postulator, Father Louis Kondor, gave Lucia several cases containing relics. In them were particles of those branches from the holm oak tree. Father Kondor knew how the branches had disappeared all those years ago, and he revealed

---

[16] *Fatima in Lucia's Own Words: Sister Lucia's Memoirs*, 16th ed. (Fatima: Secretariado dos Pastorinhos, 2007), 180.

[17] Carmel of Coimbra, *A Pathway under the Gaze of Mary* (Washington, NJ: World Apostolate of Fatima, USA, 2015), 82.

[18] Ibid.

the story to Lucia. Jacinta's father, Ti Marto, took them from under the mattress where Jacinta had put them. He held on to the branches until many years later, when he gave them to Father Kondor.

When Sister Lucia heard this story, she exclaimed with a sigh, "Well, that was very competent of Ti Marto!"[19]

Heaven always helps us along—even sometimes with events or signs for which there are no natural explanations—but only if we are open to it. Remember the famous picture of Jesus knocking at the door? There is no handle on the outside of the door. The handle is only on the inside. We have to open the door. In this case, we open it to Jesus through our Blessed Mother at Fatima and her very clear and direct instructions for us.

We've just seen how heaven helped us then, and now, through some very surprising supernatural wonders. Remember that when Jesus lived on earth and went around the countryside and through towns, He healed countless people physically—and spiritually. Why would He not heal people through His Mother's intercession at Fatima?

While countless spiritual healings took place at Fatima, especially during and after the Miracle of the Sun, there were physical healings too, such as one reported on June 18, 1918, by Father Manuel Antunes Marto to the archbishop. It concerned one of his parishioners, Maria do Carmo, of the parish of Our Lady of Light in the Diocese of Coimbra, in the district of Leiria. Father Marto had received a statement from Maria concerning her cure from tuberculosis.

Sick for five years, with her strength declining day after day, losing weight, and unable to sleep because of her severe cough,

19 Ibid.

she had no hope of recovery. Her illness had broken up her family, too, because she sent her children away, lest they become infected.

Wrote Father Marto:

> And, on being told that Our Lady had appeared to some children, [Maria] made a promise to go there on the thirteenth of four consecutive months on foot and pray on the way to see if Our Lady would cure her. The first time she went, difficult though it had been, she felt better, for the coming back was easier on her than the going. She continued to feel better all the time, and on November 13, 1917, the day she completed her promise, she found herself completely well. She attributed her cure to a miracle by Our Lady of Fatima.[20]

Healings were quite common, and the children seers were directly involved in some of them. In her memoirs, Lucia describes one healing. A young woman, about twenty years old, met the seers on their way to pray a Rosary. Crying, she "knelt down and begged us to enter her house and say at least one Hail Mary for the recovery of her father, who for three years had been unable to take any rest, on account of continual hiccoughs. In such circumstances, it was impossible to resist."[21]

Lucia helped the girl to stand up, and she recalls, "As it was already late into the night, and we were finding our way along by the light of lanterns, I therefore told Jacinta to remain there, while I went on ahead to pray the Rosary with the people, promising to call for her on my return. She agreed."[22]

[20] Martins, *Documents on Fatima*, 229.
[21] *Memoirs*, 184.
[22] Ibid.

When Lucia returned to the house, she found Jacinta in a chair and the girl's father sitting opposite her. Although not very old, he looked emaciated and cried with emotion. Relatives were gathered around him. Seeing Lucia, Jacinta stood up, offered her goodbyes, and promised that she wouldn't forget the man in her prayers.

The next morning, the children set out for a visit they had planned, and on the way they "found the happy girl accompanied by her father," Lucia recounts. "He now looked much better and had lost all trace of nervous strain and extreme weakness. They came to thank us for the grace they had received, for they said he was no longer troubled by the annoying hiccoughs."[23]

Healings like this took place without any ordinary explanation. Only heaven has the answer, and we are meant to accept the results with faith. Sometimes ordinary earth and water were the instruments for healings connected with Fatima. But this is nothing new; remember when Jesus told a blind man, "Go wash in the Pool of Siloam." The Gospel tells us, "So he went and washed, and came back able to see" (John 9:7).

The use of water in healings makes sense if we think back to the Gospels and remember that, at Lourdes, Our Lady told St. Bernadette to drink at the spring that the child saint herself had to dig—and which became a source of flowing water where people have experienced countless healings over the decades.

Likewise at Fatima: faith and ordinary substances made for plentiful healings, both physical and spiritual, and these healings multiplied after the apparitions ended. The use of these ordinary substances for healings astounded more than a few people and even got through to scoffers and atheists, turning them into believers.

---

[23] Ibid., 185.

Throughout the century following Fatima, most of the early cures of soul and body were forgotten. But Father John de Marchi recounted some of them in his classic mid-twentieth century book, *The True Story of Fatima*. Father de Marchi lived in Fatima from 1943 until 1950, researching and writing. Later he founded a seminary there. He was able to spend long hours speaking with important eyewitnesses about what they saw and experienced during and after the supernatural events of 1917.

Naturally, Father de Marchi spent lots of time with Jacinta and Francisco's parents, Manuel Pedro Marto—better known as Ti Marto—and his wife, Olimpia. He also spoke frequently with Lucia's sisters and many other people of Fatima, including Maria Carreira—better known as Maria da Capelinha, or Mary of the Chapel, who was custodian of the Chapel of the Apparitions and of the first statue of Our Lady of Fatima to be placed there. Her son John was also the sacristan of the chapel. Father de Marchi calls Maria "among my most indispensable assistants."[24]

To top this all off, Father de Marchi notes that the content of his book "has been checked for truth and exact detail by Lucia,"[25] who at the time was a Carmelite nun. Lucia and Father de Marchi were friends and knew each other well from the time she was a Dorothean Sister.

Put all these impeccable witnesses together, and there's not the slightest question concerning the miracles they saw and described.

Father de Marchi recounts some incidents shared with him by Maria da Capelinha. In one case, a poor woman traveled from her home in Tomar to Fatima, a distance of about twenty-four

[24] De Marchi, *True Story*, 3.
[25] Ibid., 2.

miles, to get some earth from the apparition site. She was among others who came to dig up earth near the holm oak tree and use it in the hope of curing sick people. Some sick had even consumed this earth and got better right afterward. It may sound rather unusual, but consider this example.

Maria gave the specifics:

> In Alqueidao (forty-five miles away) there was a girl who had been paralyzed for seven months. Her parents did not have her treated, and she was very poor. One day Our Lady of Fatima appeared to her and told her that she would cure her if her mother would go to the Cova and take some earth from under the oak tree and eat some of it during a novena. It all happened as Our Lady had said, and the girl was perfectly cured.[26]

Another time, Maria approached a man from Torres Novas (twenty-three miles away) who was near one of the oak trees, crying. When she asked what was troubling him, he told her about the open wound he had had on his leg for twenty-four years "which was always full of pus and prevented him from working or even moving because it would never heal." The man told her:

> My wife came to Fatima and took away some earth to make an infusion to wash my wound with. I did not want her to do this because the wound needed cleanliness, and the mud would certainly make it worse. But my wife, who had great faith, said that many people had been cured with the earth, and although I had no faith at all in God nor any religion, she insisted so much that at last I let

---

[26] Ibid., 178.

her have her way. Every day for nine days she washed the wound with that mud, and each day it healed a little more, until at the end of the novena it was perfectly cured. I burst into tears, took off the bandages, and came here on foot although I couldn't move before![27]

This is a good example of why Our Lady came to us at Fatima. She wanted people to be healed not only physically, but in the greatest way of all—spiritually. Didn't Christ do that when He cured the man at the pool of Bethesda and then told him, "Look, you are well; do not sin any more, so that nothing worse may happen to you" (John 5:14)? And similarly with the woman whom He prevented from being stoned when He said to her, "Go, [and] from now on do not sin any more" (John 8:11)?

Maria da Capelinha related similar story about a man from Tomar who was an unbeliever and suffering from tuberculosis. He explained to Maria that his wife told him they would travel to Fatima to "make a novena and drink an infusion of the earth from under the tree where Our Lady had appeared." But the man had refused. When his wife would not accept his refusal, he gave in and "consented to drink the infusion, though without faith or devotion. In spite of this, Our Lady cured him, and in a few days, he was strong and healthy again." He, too, had come to his spiritual senses.[28]

After the healings started in Fatima, people arrived every day to get some of the earth from the Cova near the spot of the apparitions. They came hoping for cures of physical ailments and of all sorts of other problems. Many made pilgrimages during the

---

[27] Ibid.

[28] Ibid., 179.

1918 influenza pandemic that was sweeping the world. Either they were already sick, or they were frightened of catching this deadly flu.

Maria related that the people would process with images of Our Lady of the Rosary and of their favorite saints. A priest named Friar David from nearby, whom Maria called a wise and good man, came and gave the first sermon at the Cova. In it, he stressed that the important thing to pursue was "amendment of life." Already very sick, Jacinta was present at the Cova on that day.

"[The] people were weeping in sorrow over this epidemic. Our Lady heard the prayers they offered," Maria told Father de Marchi, "because from that day on, we had no more cases of influenza in our district."[29] From then on, as you might expect, devotion to Our Lady of Fatima grew even greater, and after the chapel was built, thousands and thousands more came. The people took away spoonfuls of earth in handkerchiefs or in paper, and later they were able to make use of another vehicle for healing—water found in the Cova.

There had been no water at the Cova from the time of the apparitions. Then, on the bishop of Leiria's first visit to the Cova, after Jacinta and Francisco had died, he saw how dry the whole place was and told Maria da Capelinha's husband to dig a well. Pilgrims coming there in increasing numbers would need water.

Before the first day of digging was over, the workers hit rock. But when they blasted the rock, water flowed out generously.

Daily, people filled bottles and pitchers with the water and took it to those who were ill so that they could drink it or wash

---

[29] Ibid.

their wounds with it. Father de Marchi repeated this testimony given by resident Jose Alves:

> Everyone had the greatest faith in Our Lady's water, and she used it to cure their wounds and their pains. Never did Our Lady perform so many miracles as at that time. I saw people with terrible legs that were running with pus, but when they washed themselves with the water, they were able to leave their bandages behind because Our Lady had cured them. Other people knelt down and drank that earthy water and were cured of serious internal diseases.[30]

Miracles became bountiful. Father de Marchi personally witnessed just about every kind of physical cure that occurred there.

"We who have had the privilege of living close beside the Cova da Iria do not face the problem of merely believing in Mary's powers of intercession," he wrote.[31] He and others living near the Cova were able to witness her powers.

Father de Marchi remarks:

> There is clinical certainty that at Fatima the blind have had sight restored, while men and women stretcher-borne have risen from their litters to cry hosannas to the Power that can in one moment banish cancer, loosen the fist of the tightest paralysis, or render whole and clean the shrunken lungs of abandoned tuberculars. More than a hundred contradictions of the natural physical law have been registered at Fatima and held to be valid only after the most exhaustive and scrupulous examination of all available evidence.[32]

---

[30] Ibid., 180.
[31] Ibid., 182.
[32] Ibid., 6.

The Fruits of Fatima

While Father de Marchi counted it as a divine gift to have been present for so many miraculous healings, he also stated, "To those who do not require the spangles of visible prodigy to know that God is in His heaven, the spiritual message of Fatima remains of infinitely greater importance."[33]

Most significantly, he pointed out that all these physical cures, as phenomenal as they were, were minor compared to the great number of souls Our Lady was harvesting for Jesus, her Son. All people need only to listen to her in order to be healed. Why?

"At Fatima," he said, "the world has received, through Mary, God's own prescription for peace."[34] The biggest miracles will happen when we put into practice what Our Lady of Fatima, Our Lady of the Rosary, told us and asked us to do.

Cures connected to Fatima began to happen on an international scale, too, years after the apparitions. Everybody has surely heard of this next person who attributed his healing to Our Lady of Fatima: St. Padre Pio.

While countless people know of him, few know that he was very seriously ill, bedridden, and Our Lady of Fatima visited him at San Giovanni Rotondo to cure him. She made this special trip to help a favorite son who was thoroughly devoted to her Fatima messages.

The miraculous event happened in 1959. That spring, the pilgrim statue of Our Lady of Fatima had come from Portugal to make several stops around Italy's provincial capitals. Traveling by helicopter, the statue was en route to Foggia, where Bishop Paolo Carta had readied a tremendous welcome for Our Lady. But she took a detour.

[33] Ibid.
[34] Ibid.

Later in 1997, as bishop emeritus, Carta would tell the story and a bit about the longtime love Padre Pio had for Our Lady of Fatima in *Voice of Padre Pio* from the Friary of Our Lady of Grace, in San Giovanni Rotondo.

In his writings, Bishop Carta recalls the requests of Our Lady at Fatima and says, "In the half century which followed, no one in the Church has given a more complete reply than Padre Pio. The maternal anxiety of the Immaculate Heart of Mary for the souls going to hell had profoundly and completely invaded the heart of Padre Pio, who made of his whole life a great sacrifice to our Lord to snatch souls away from eternal damnation."[35]

The bishop notes that, at Fatima, Our Lady asked especially for the Rosary. "And who could count the hours Padre Pio spent in prayer for the conversion and salvation of sinners?" he says. "And with how much loving insistence did he not recommend the Rosary to everyone as a means of salvation?"

Further, the bishop points to the countless acts of mortification, penances, and sufferings to save souls from hell that Padre Pio practiced in answer to what Our Lady had called for. "This heroic reply of Padre Pio's deserved a sign of maternal pleasure from Our Lady. And the sign was marvelous," he writes.

The monastery in San Giovanni Rotondo was within the Foggia Diocese, where the pilgrim statue of Our Lady of Fatima from Portugal was scheduled to stop. But Padre Pio had been severely ill with pleurisy for months, unable even to celebrate Mass, let alone go to Foggia. Now it was the beginning of

---

[35] All quotations are from Bishop Paola Carta, "Padre Pio and the Immaculate Heart of Mary," from *Voice of Padre Pio* (San Giovanni Rotondo: Friary of Our Lady of Grace 1997), www.ewtn.com/padrepio/mystic/Mary.htm.

August, when Mary was to arrive, and Padre Pio remained bedridden.

"But could the Mother with an Immaculate Heart so sensitive and delicate not visit her dearest son, Padre Pio?" explained Bishop Carta.

Somehow the schedule got changed. Now the statue would not go to Foggia but to San Giovanni Rotondo instead. Joy filled the air as people gathered by the monastery. With the help of a loudspeaker, Padre Pio was able to prepare them for their Mother's arrival on August 6.

On the morning of August 6, Padre Pio managed to get to the church. He approached the statue of Our Lady "but had to sit down because he was exhausted—and he gave her a gold rosary," observes Bishop Carta. "The statue was lowered before his face and he was able to kiss her. It was a most affectionate gesture."

That same afternoon, between two and three o'clock, Our Lady of Fatima was again on the helicopter, ready to travel to the next stop. Taking off from the House for the Relief of the Suffering—which was built because of Padre Pio's idea and inspiration and opened on May 5, 1956—the helicopter circled three times around the monastery before flying away to its next stop. Afterward, the pilot could never explain why that circling happened.

Bishop Carta describes the departure of the statue, saying, "From a window Padre Pio watched the helicopter fly away with eyes filled with tears. To Our Lady in flight Padre Pio lamented with a confidence that was all his own: 'My Lady, my Mother, you came to Italy, and I got sick; now you are going away, and you leave me still ill.'"

But as the helicopter was circling, he felt a shudder, a jolt, through his body. Bishop Carta repeats what Padre Pio would say about the incident for the rest of his life: "In that very instant I felt a sort of shudder in my bones which cured me immediately." The bishop adds the words of Padre Pio's spiritual father, who confirmed the event: "In a moment, the Padre felt a mysterious force in his body and said to his confreres: 'I am cured.' He was healthy and strong as never before in his life."

In *Padre Pio: A Personal Portrait*, originally published in 1978 and republished in 2016, Friar Francesco Napolitano, who worked with the saintly friar, said, "I was present at the scene and can testify that Padre Pio never felt as healthy as he did after the departure of the statue of Our Lady of Fatima."

When Padre Pio was told about an article in the Foggia paper, which asked why Our Lady of Fatima went to San Giovanni Rotondo instead of the shrine of St. Michael at Monte Sant'Angelo in Foggia, Bishop Carta writes that Padre Pio simply replied, "Our Lady came here because she wanted to cure Padre Pio." Three days after her visit, he was back to celebrating Mass.

Bishop Carta also shares his own idea of why Our Lady of Fatima came to Padre Pio's monastery: "I like to add that she also came because the example of Padre Pio's ardent devotion and his prodigious recovery would rouse in Italy and the world a fervent increase of love and confidence towards the Immaculate Heart of Mary."

Bishop Carta saw this heavenly favor as a reminder, adding:

From this marvelous episode we must make a holy resolution to grow always in this devotion with a generous reply to the message of Fatima, reciting fervently the Rosary every day, praying and offering our sufferings for the conversion of sinners, receiving Communion on the first Saturdays of the month in the hope that the consoling words will come true for us: "I promise salvation to all those who practice devotion to my Immaculate Heart. These souls will be most dear to God, and like flowers I will place them before his throne."[36]

For his most devout response to Our Lady's message and requests, Padre Pio is like a whole bouquet.

The wonders, cures, and phenomena abounding in the days during and following the Fatima apparitions, whether soon after or decades later, continuously proclaim the importance of that message, on which heaven threw a spotlight, focusing in on it, and putting rows of exclamation points after it. These wonders are meant to lead us to faith and, more specifically, to respond to what Our Lady of Fatima asks of us for our good and the good of the world—to put her message into practice in our lives. We'll touch on this subject in greater detail in upcoming chapters. First, though, let's look at one more miraculous event that amplifies the supernatural character of Fatima yet again.

Of course, we know that heaven can give any kind of a sign or confirmation concerning an event like the great apparitions of Our Lady at Fatima. But we must be sure to open our minds and hearts to them and not get pulled into the skepticism of this scientific and technological age. An excellent example of one such sign happened over several days in 1946.

Nineteen forty-six was a banner year for Fatima and for the whole country, which was celebrating the three hundredth anniversary of the Blessed Virgin Mary reigning as Queen of Portugal. She received that title in 1646, when King João IV took the crown off his own head and placed it at the feet of a statue

---

[36] Also in Cappa, *Fatima: Cove of Wonders*, 273.

of Our Lady, declaring her to be the Queen and Patroness of Portugal under the title of the Immaculate Conception. No king after him reclaimed the crown because João IV's action made it unquestionably the Blessed Virgin Mary's crown.

The year 1946 also marked another crowning of the Blessed Mother — as Our Lady of Fatima. On May 13, Cardinal Benedetto Masella officially represented Pope Pius XII and crowned the statue of Our Lady of Fatima at the Cova da Iria. The women of Portugal had donated all the jewels that adorned this crown. Nearly three-quarters of a million people were there for the ceremony.

Then came a third major event in December, specifically set for December 8, the feast of the Immaculate Conception. On that day, the statue of Our Lady of Fatima would be crowned again in Lisbon's Sé Velha Cathedral by Cardinal Manuel Gonçalves Cerejeira, who would also renew the consecration of Portugal to the Immaculate Conception.

This world-famous statue would not simply be driven over to the cathedral but would be the center of attention for what amounted to a national pilgrimage and procession, beginning on November 22 at Fatima and lasting two weeks. The walk from there to the Lisbon cathedral was more than eighty miles. As teams of men carried the statue, hails to Our Lady and formal and informal receptions of her came at every step of the route and in every town along the way. There were religious and civil services, too. Never was Our Lady left alone overnight either. She spent the nights in well-attended churches that hosted continuous vigils.

Doves joined the procession at about the halfway mark, at Bombarral, forty-five miles from Lisbon.

Father Thomas McGlynn, a Dominican who was in Portugal sculpting a statue of Our Lady of Fatima in consultation with

Sister Lucia, related that a woman who was living in Bombarral had bought six white doves at the market. One died, leaving five doves, which the woman gave to two small girls who were to release them as an act of devotion before the statue of Our Lady. They did. Two doves flew away, but a trinity of them "flew to the statue and settled in the flowers at its feet."[37]

People tried to chase them away, but the triumvirate paid no attention. Whenever they were forced away, they quickly returned to their station. Finally, the doves won. The people relented, convinced to let the trio stay because of its remarkable determination. And stay they did over the five-day walk from that city to the Lisbon cathedral. The doves remained steadfast and peaceful at the base of the statue at Our Lady's feet or cozy in the flowers near her.

What's more, nothing bothered them. In one of his books, John Haffert cites a priest named Father Oliveira, who witnessed the three doves:

> Bands played, people shouted, the bier on which the statue was mounted moved and swayed, rockets exploded at night and cascaded fire, while giant searchlights burned at them. They were constantly buffeted by flowers tossed to the statue from the surging crowds. But they did not fly. They blinked, shook off flowers that hit them, occasionally stretched their wings to keep balance. But they remained there at her feet during the entire two-week journey. They refused food or drink.[38]

---

[37] Fr. Thomas McGlynn, O.P., *Vision of Fatima* (Manchester, NH: Sophia Institute Press, 2017), 164.

[38] Haffert, *Russia Will Be Converted*, 197–198.

There was more to come.

Arriving in Lisbon, the procession first headed to the new parish of the Church of Our Lady of Fatima, where they would remain for ceremonies and Mass until the evening of December 7, when Our Lady would be processed through the city to the Sé, Lisbon's cathedral.

"The cardinal met the procession at the church door and delivered an address welcoming the Queen of Portugal to the capital," wrote Father McGlynn. When he spoke, the doves flew by the cardinal, looking at him "as if they were listening to and understanding what he was saying."[39]

The doves remained at Our Lady's feet all that night of December 5. Then at the Solemn Mass to follow, another phenomenon took place, beginning at the elevation of the Host. Father Oliveira describes it best:

> To the utter amazement of all, two of the doves suddenly flew ... after two weeks of refusing food or drink and of remaining at the feet of the statue.... One sped straight to the gospel side of the altar, and the other to the epistle side! There, as the bishop straightened to raise the consecrated Host, they alighted and folded their wings ... one on each side ... as though in adoration! As the Mass progressed, the two doves remained there to the bewilderment of the celebrants and servers and the stupefied congregation. But this was still not the climax. The third dove had not left the statue. Suddenly, at the moment of Communion, the third dove flew up and perched on top of the statue's golden crown ... and as the celebrant

---

[39] McGlynn, *Vision of Fatima*, 165.

turned and held up Our Lord, saying, "Ecce Agnus Dei" (Behold the Lamb of God), it spread its white wings and held them open!"[40]

For the next two days the statue of Our Lady remained in the church named in her honor—Our Lady of Fatima.

On the evening of December 7, everyone was readying for the huge procession to begin at 10 p.m., and what the doves did next was described by Cardinal Cerejeira:

> When the image of Our Lady was about to leave the Church of Our Lady of Fatima on its way to the Sé [the cathedral], in the most glorious acclamation ever given to a queen of Portugal, we saw two little doves that, since Bombarral, nothing could move from the image, poised on the edge of a stained glass window—that of the angels in glory, which surrounds the Throne of Exposition—closely joined together, immobile, and turned toward the image, as if saying farewell to the image and to their faithful companion at its feet.[41]

As Our Lady left the church, the heavy rain that evening stopped like a faucet being shut off. The sky became clear, and the moon appeared. It seemed to be a visual reminder of the prayer from the Legion of Mary, derived from Song of Songs 6:10: "Who is she that comes forth as the morning rising, fair as the moon, bright as the sun, terrible as an army set in battle array?"

An estimated five hundred thousand people lined the nearly four-mile route to the cathedral. Myriads more watched from

---

[40] Haffert, *Russia Will Be Converted*, 198–199.

[41] McGlynn, *Vision of Fatima*, 165–166.

windows along the route. Everybody saw the honor guard of the three doves.

As planned, the procession with Our Lady of Fatima arrived at the cathedral shortly after midnight on December 8, Mary's feast day. All night long, people filed into the church, praying without end.

In the morning, the cardinal celebrated a Pontifical Mass, and in the afternoon, he renewed the consecration of Portugal to the Immaculate Conception. Portugal's church hierarchy, Portugal's president, and every one of the country's high officials attended this major religious event.

The symbolic presence of the doves was not lost on the on-lookers either. Father McGlynn observed that Cardinal Cerejeira was joined by others who all were well aware of the symbolism surrounding doves in the Christian tradition, drawing attention to the dove of Noah's ark, which is symbolic of peace, and also the dove at the baptism of Our Lord. Jesus used doves as symbols of the virtues of simplicity, innocence, meekness. The three doves suggested the Three Persons of the Blessed Trinity, the three theological virtues, and the three Fatima children. The number three in this case could also stand for the three centuries of Portugal's consecration to the Immaculate Conception, which the doves of Bombarral so beautifully helped celebrate in December 1946.

That symbolism and the story of the doves were remembered and represented through the years, especially with the International Pilgrim Virgin Statue of Our Lady of Fatima—the one that has visited the United Nations twice, the second time in 2017. It includes three doves carved at the feet of Our Lady to recall that wondrous event witnessed by scores of people in Portugal but now not often remembered as it should be.

2

The Three Visions Following
the Miracle of the Sun

Anyone who has heard of Fatima is normally familiar with the Miracle of the Sun to some degree and therefore knows at least something about the miraculous movement of the sun that day. But even after people saw the sun return to its normal place in the sky, the wonders did not end. Next came three visual teachings from Our Lady and heaven — now mostly forgotten or sidelined. They were — and remain — however, full of essential teachings about Fatima. Even more, we need to respond to Our Lady and bring these major teachings into our spiritual lives.

These three visions were presented without words. They were silent. But they conveyed teachings of the utmost importance. They must be recalled. They must be remembered. They must be followed.

Lucia, in fact, stressed their importance many times. "God chose to conclude the Message in Fatima, on October 1917, with three further apparitions which I regard as three more calls placed before us," she wrote in her book *"Calls" from the Message of Fatima.* She and her two saintly cousins saw these visions as "significant apparitions."[42]

Let's look at each one of them and what they tell us.

To begin, in her memoirs, Sister Lucia describes these three visions immediately following the Miracle of the Sun. Back in September, Our Lady had prepared the children for her October 13 appearance and what they would see then. Our Lady did not want to give the children any last-minute surprises. She said, "In October, Our Lord will come, as well as Our Lady of Dolors (Sorrows) and Our Lady of Carmel. St. Joseph will appear with the Child Jesus to bless the world."[43]

Not only would Our Lady come as she had five previous times, but this time she would be there under three titles. Obviously, she chose the titles because she wanted to tell the children (and always remember, she meant this by extension for all of us, not just for the three seers) what devotions to her would please heaven at this time — and how those devotions would help each one of us and the world. That is why she came to Fatima and what she made clear in all her previous visits to the children.

Lucia describes the three visions that she, Jacinta, and Francisco witnessed following the Miracle of the Sun. She writes about seeing "St. Joseph with the Child Jesus and Our Lady, robed in white with a blue mantle, beside the sun. St. Joseph and the Child Jesus appeared to bless the world, for they traced the Sign of the Cross with their hands."[44]

---

[42] Sister Maria Lucia of Jesus and of the Immaculate Heart, *"Calls" from the Message of Fatima* (Fatima: Secretariado dos Pastorinhos, 2000), 164.

[43] *Memoirs*, 181.

[44] Ibid., 183.

Lucia describes Our Lord and Our Lady appearing next. She writes, "It seemed to me that it was Our Lady of Dolors (Sorrows). Our Lord appeared to bless the world in the same manner as St. Joseph had done."[45]

When this apparition vanished, she "saw Our Lady once more, this time resembling Our Lady of Carmel." Our Lady was emphasizing to all of us the importance of the brown scapular. Lucia later affirmed, "The scapular and the Rosary are inseparable. The scapular is a sign of consecration to Our Lady."[46] And devotion (and consecration) to the Immaculate Heart is one of the "must-do's," as Our Lady taught in the June and July apparitions.

So, what do the visions mean? In her book *"Calls" from the Message of Fatima*, written when she was a Carmelite, Sister Lucia has much to say about what God wished to tell us with the apparitions—that is why she titled her book and explained them as the "calls" of Fatima.

Looking at these three visions, let's absorb the easy lessons that they teach us and consider what they call us to do.

The Vision of the Holy Family

The vision of the Holy Family appearing together after the Miracle of the Sun on October 13 surely spoke of what was coming if people didn't heed Fatima's calls. In the latter half of the twentieth century, focusing on this first vision—Our Lady and the Child Jesus in the arms of St. Joseph, blessing the people—Lucia wrote, "In times such as the present, when the family often seems

---

45 Ibid.
46 Fr. Kilian Lynch, O. Carm., *Our Lady of Fatima and the Brown Scapular*, 4th ed. (Faversham, Kent, England: Carmelite Press, 1980), 15.

misunderstood in the form in which it was established by God and is assailed by doctrines that are erroneous and contrary to the purposes for which the Divine Creator instituted it, surely God wished to address to us a reminder of the purpose for which He established the family in the world."[47]

Pointing out various Scripture passages, she said:

> God entrusted to the family the sacred mission of cooperating with Him in the work of creation. This decision to associate His poor creatures with His creative work is a great demonstration of the fatherly goodness of God.... Thus the Divine Creator wished to entrust to the family a sacred mission that makes two beings become one in union so close that it does not admit of separation. It is from this union that God wishes to produce other beings.... God established Matrimony as an indissoluble union.[48]

Family holiness is essential. Lucia said this in the later 1990s, and in 1981, she wrote in a letter to Cardinal Carlo Caffarra a dire warning he revealed in 2008, which we see rapidly unfolding in the world: "The final battle between the Lord and the kingdom of Satan will be about marriage and the family. Don't be afraid.... Whoever works for the sanctity of marriage and the family will always be fought against and opposed in every way, because this is the decisive issue." She ended by saying, "Nevertheless, Our Lady has already crushed his head."[49]

---

[47] "Calls," 162.

[48] Ibid., 162–163.

[49] Catholic News Agency, "Fatima Visionary Predicted 'Final Battle' Would Be over Marriage, Family," December 31, 2016,

St. John Paul II also saw what was coming for society and the family. In 1981, in *Familiaris Consortio*, he noted that the times were "a moment of history in which the family is the object of numerous forces that seek to destroy it or in some way to deform it." He listed and named the attacks that we see now unfolding in full force. Simultaneously, he stressed that "the well-being of society and her own good are intimately tied to the good of the family."[50]

Earlier, on Holy Family Sunday in 1978, the pope strongly stated that the family "constitutes the primary, fundamental, and irreplaceable community for man." And he stressed, "The mission of being the primary vital cell of society has been given to the family by God Himself."[51]

The vision of the Holy Family at Fatima on October 13, 1917, was to remind us of this reality. John Paul II noted that the Church celebrates the feast of the Holy Family during Christmastide "to recall that the fundamental values, which cannot be violated without incalculable harm of a moral nature, are bound up with the family."[52]

"The family of Nazareth ... really constitutes that culminating point of reference for the holiness of every human family," the Holy Father emphasized.[53]

---

https://www.catholicnewsagency.com/news/fatima-visionary-predicted-final-battle-would-be-over-marriage-family-17760.

[50] John Paul II, Apostolic Exhortation *Familiaris Consortio* (November 22, 1981), no. 3.

[51] John Paul II, Homily, Church of the Most Holy Name of Jesus, December 31, 1978.

[52] Ibid.

[53] Ibid.

The Fruits of Fatima

In his Angelus on December 31, 2000, he again reminded of many attacks on the family and concluded, "All this shows how urgent it is to rediscover the value of the family and to help it in every way to be, as God wanted it, the vital environment where every child who comes into the world is welcomed with tenderness and gratitude from the moment of his conception; a place marked by a serene atmosphere that encourages the harmonious human and spiritual development of all its members."[54]

Then, in his 2001 Angelus on Holy Family Sunday, the saintly Holy Father again emphasized, "The Redeemer of the world chose the family as the place for his birth and growth, thereby sanctifying this fundamental institution of every society."[55]

Sister Lucia was of the same mind. Reflecting on the family after seeing the Holy Family at Fatima, she writes, "God established Matrimony as an indissoluble union. Once a couple have received the sacrament of Matrimony, the union between the two is definitive and cannot be broken; it is indissoluble as long as the couple remain alive."[56]

She also noted the very clear and simple reason — "God ordained it to be" — citing proof in Genesis 2:24, "which Jesus Christ confirmed and endorsed in Matthew 19:4–6, in the face of human efforts, at that time, to pull in the opposite direction."[57]

According to Lucia, becoming one in the bond of love, commitment, and cooperation with God in the work of creation "involves the sacrifice and immolation that the giving of oneself

---

[54] John Paul II, Angelus, December 31, 2000.

[55] John Paul II, Angelus, December 20, 2001.

[56] "Calls," 163.

[57] Ibid.

always implies," and it also involves "mutual understanding, forgiveness, and pardon. It is thus that a home is built up, made holy, and gives glory to God."[58]

Of course, we know that is not quite what the secular world—from television, to movies, to magazines, to newspapers, to the Internet—drills into us 24–7. It's quite the opposite, in fact.

Yet, in his 1978 Holy Family homily, John Paul II noted these insights brought out by Lucia when he spoke on these fundamental values. The first "is the value of the person which is expressed in absolute mutual faithfulness until death," and the second is "the personal value of the new life ... of the child, from the first moment of his conception."[59]

In this first vision on October 13, 1917, right after the Miracle of the Sun, surely Our Lady and heaven were telling us to make the family strong; to build the family not on sandy secular soil but on rock-solid ground, as God intended it. If not, the family would suffer when the storms would come. It's obvious what happened, as people did not listen and respond in large numbers. But Lucia's warnings and John Paul II's writings on the family were there to caution people once again, to counsel them, and to light the right path to take.

Lucia wrote much about the family. She reminded parents that they have a duty to their children, and children that they have a duty to their parents.

A primary duty for parents, Lucia said, is to instill a knowledge of God and His commandments at an early age, teaching children to "keep them in mind and to observe them." Parents

---

[58] Ibid.
[59] John Paul II, Homily, Church of the Most Holy Name of Jesus, December 31, 1978.

who don't do this fail "to fulfill the mission entrusted to them by God."[60] And she quoted Deuteronomy 6:5–7, in which parents are told, "Therefore, you shall love the LORD, your God, with your whole heart, and with your whole being, and with your whole strength. Take to heart these words which I command you today. Keep repeating them to your children. Recite them when you are at home and when you are away, when you lie down and when you get up."

Like Pope John Paul II, Lucia was not afraid to warn transgressors, either. She writes, "Parents who disregard this law of God make themselves responsible for the ignorance that is responsible for the disordered lives of the children who torment the declining years of their parents, and are themselves lost." For their sublime and solemn mission, parents "are answerable to God."[61]

The Fatima seer stressed how essential it is for parents to guide

> their children's first steps to the altar of God, teaching them to raise their innocent hands and to pray, helping them to discover how to find God on their way and to follow the echo of His voice. This is the most serious and important mission that has been entrusted by God to parents; and they must fulfill it so well that throughout their lives, the memory of their parents will always arouse in their children the memory of God and of His teaching.[62]

What about the children? Are they off the hook? Not from what Lucia had to say.

[60] "Calls," 164.
[61] Ibid.
[62] Ibid.

"The children," Lucia says, "must never forget or set to one side the respect, gratitude, and help which they owe to their parents, who are for them the image of God."[63]

As parents sacrifice themselves to raise, educate, and establish their children in life, children are, in turn, duty-bound also to sacrifice in order "to give pleasure, joy, and serenity to their parents, aiding and assisting them, if necessary, in such a way that everything is done out of true love and with one's eyes fixed on God."[64]

Again, in his 1978 Holy Family homily, John Paul II pointed out that the Gospel "shows us, very clearly, the educative aspect of the family," referring to twelve-year-old Jesus in relation to Mary and Joseph, and how he "was obedient to them."[65]

It's an example for children, of course. "This submission, obedience, readiness to accept the mature examples of the human conduct of the family, is necessary, on the part of children and of the young generation," confirmed John Paul II. "And parents must measure their whole conduct with this 'obedience,' this readiness of the child to accept the examples of human behavior. This is the particularly delicate point of their responsibility as parents, of their responsibility with regard to the man, this little and then growing man entrusted to them by God himself."

The vision of the Holy Family at Fatima was already giving us this example, laying the groundwork, so to speak, for what they knew would be these necessary, strong reminders that would come decades later from Lucia, John Paul II, and others. And

---

[63] Ibid., 165.

[64] Ibid., 165–166.

[65] John Paul II, Homily, Church of the Most Holy Name of Jesus, December 31, 1978.

necessarily so if people did not heed the Fatima messages and teachings.

John Paul II warned that material, economic, and social views often prevailed over Christian principles and morality.

"The future of humanity passes through the family," he stated in *Familiaris Consortio* (75). With that being the case, what does the family need to do to protect the future of humanity? John Paul II had the answer: "The Church relies especially on the witness and contribution of Christian families to fulfil her urgent mission. Indeed, in the face of the dangers and difficulties that beset the family institution, she invites families to have greater spiritual and apostolic boldness, knowing that the family is called to be 'a sign of unity for the world' and thus to bear witness to 'the Kingdom and peace of Christ.' "[66]

So how can the family model itself on the Holy Family? Big hint: six times in *Familiaris Consortio*, John Paul II calls the family "the domestic church." And in his 2001 Holy Family Sunday Angelus, he reminded, "The humble dwelling place in Nazareth is *an authentic school of the Gospel*. Here we admire, put into practice, the divine plan to make the family an *intimate community of life and love*; here we learn that every Christian family is called to be a small *'domestic church'* that must shine with the Gospel virtues."[67]

In the first Fatima vision, heaven was already reminding us of this truth.

In *Familiaris Consortio*, we also learn that "only with God's unceasing aid, which will surely be granted if it is humbly and trustingly petitioned in prayer," will families rise to responsibility

---

[66] John Paul II, Angelus, December 30, 2001, no. 3.
[67] Ibid., no. 2.

as the domestic church (59). A major help is Our Lady, "Mother of Christian families, of domestic Churches" (61). Pick up the Rosary, as Fatima taught us.

Years earlier, in one of his radio messages, Pope Pius XII emphasized that "the Virgin Mother's insistence on the recitation of the family Rosary was meant to teach us that the secret of peace in family life lies in imitating the virtues of the Holy Family."[68]

See how Fatima, in its visions and messages on that October 13, was already giving us a visual broadcast of all this?

Fatima seer Sister Lucia has a beautiful way of describing the holy families that we are called to be:

> A home must be like a garden, where fresh rosebuds are opening, bringing to the world the freshness of innocence, a pure and trusting outlook on life, and the smile of innocent happy children. Only thus does God take pleasure in His creative work, blessing it and turning His fatherly gaze upon it. Any other way of behaving is to divert the work of God from its end, to alter the plans of God, failing to fulfill and carry out the mission that God has entrusted to the married couple.[69]

Looking to the apparitions, she concluded that "in the Message of Fatima, God calls on us to turn our eyes to the Holy Family of Nazareth, into which He chose to be born, and to grow in grace and stature, in order to present to us a model

[68] Fr. John A. Hardon, S.J., "Pope Pius XII and Our Lady," *Review for Religious* 11 (September 1952): 249–256, Real Presence Association, www.therealpresence.org/archives/Mariology/Mariology_005.htm.

[69] "*Calls*," 163.

to imitate, as our footsteps tread the path of our pilgrimage to heaven."[70]

From any angle, we can see that's the simple summary of the Holy Family's message.

The Vision of Our Lady of Mount Carmel and the Brown Scapular

The Fatima apparitions call us to renew our devotion to Our Lady through the brown scapular as well as the Rosary; the two go hand-in-hand. This tip-off also came during the October 13 apparition.

On that day, Mary first identified herself as Our Lady of the Rosary. Following the Miracle of the Sun, she also appeared as Our Lady of Sorrows and Our Lady of Mount Carmel, holding and offering a brown scapular.

Mary first gave the scapular to St. Simon Stock on July 16, 1251, in Aylesford, England. "Take this scapular, it shall be a sign of salvation, a protection in danger and a pledge of peace. Whosoever dies wearing this scapular shall not suffer eternal fire," our Blessed Mother promised Simon Stock, the prior general of the Carmelite order.

Over the years, devotion to the scapular grew as it became clear that this sacramental and devotion was universal. The Church eventually began celebrating the feast of Our Lady of Mount Carmel on July 16. Interestingly, Our Lady's last apparition to St. Bernadette at Lourdes in 1858 took place on July 16, her feast day. It was like a little introduction several years before Fatima.

---

[70] Ibid.

Furthermore, it's no coincidence that our Blessed Mother gave us the Rosary and the scapular in the same century. There's that number thirteen again.

The Carmelites have always been Our Lady's devoted servants. Yet she did not give the scapular just to the Carmelites. She gave it to the whole world so that all her children can wear this "habit" as an outward sign of her love for them. Mary herself chose this garment for us.

Look at Pope St. John Paul II's scapular-Fatima connection. It's another clear tip-off.

When John Paul II was shot on May 13, 1981, the feast of Our Lady of Fatima, he firmly directed the doctors not to remove his brown scapular. "And the surgeons left it on," Father Mariano Cera reported in *Inside the Vatican* magazine.[71]

John Paul II's devotion to the scapular began in childhood and continued. A photo taken during a work break with coworkers before he was ordained shows young factory worker Karol Wojtyla wearing a very visible brown scapular.

In a letter to the Carmelites, John Paul II wrote that "the most genuine form of devotion to the Most Holy Virgin, expressed by the humble sign of the scapular, is the consecration to her Immaculate Heart."[72]

See how the scapular also ties into another major request at Fatima — the consecration to Mary's Immaculate Heart? Let's keep that in the forefront of our minds and hearts.

---

[71] "The Scapular Devotion of John Paul II," Order of Carmelites, www.ocarm.org/en/content/ocarm/scapular-devotion-pope-john-paul-ii.

[72] John Paul II, Message to the Carmelite Family (March 25, 2001), no. 4.

The Fruits of Fatima

The scapular is "a tangible symbol of the deeper reality of Mary clothing and protecting us with her own mantle of protection," said Carmelite Father Justin Francis Cinnante at the National Shrine of Our Lady of Mount Carmel. "The scapular is a miniature habit of the order."[73] And this mini habit confers the same privileges Mary gave the order.

"It's not just physical miracles that take place under Our Lady's mantle," Father Cinnante continued, "but how many times we're protected from the Evil One through the scapular."[74]

The Vatican's *Directory on Popular Piety* also has very clear teachings on the brown scapular for the Church. It notes, "The scapular is an external sign of the filial relationship established between the Blessed Virgin Mary, Mother and Queen of Mount Carmel, and the faithful who entrust themselves totally to her protection, who have recourse to her maternal intercession, who are mindful of the primacy of the spiritual life and the need for prayer."[75]

The directory defines the scapular as "truly universal" and, without doubt, a pious practice the Magisterium has continuously recommended through the centuries. When we wear it with reverence and understanding of its meaning, we can be sure that the Blessed Mother will protect us continuously.

---

[73] Joseph Pronechen, "Powerful Brown Scapular and Its Perennial Promises," *National Catholic Register*, July 16, 2018, www.ncregister.com/blog/joseph-pronechen/powerful-brown-scapular-and-its-perennial-promises.

[74] Ibid.

[75] Congregation for Divine Worship and the Discipline of the Sacraments, *Directory on Popular Piety and the Liturgy* (December 2001), no. 205.

That is why saints have also known the scapular "is a sign feared by Satan and is a 'buckler' or defense against the powers of evil. [76]

What did Lucia have to say about the scapular and its connection to the Rosary and Fatima?

In 1950, Carmelite Father Kilian Lynch, the prior of Aylesford, traveled to Coimbra to speak with Sister Lucia about the brown scapular and its place within the Fatima message. In his small book, *Our Lady of Fatima and the Brown Scapular*, he recounts two major conversations that Lucia had with other Carmelite priests, addressing these questions.

In 1949, Father Donald O'Callaghan asked Lucia for her interpretation of Our Lady coming as Our Lady of Mount Carmel. Her interpretation was that "the scapular devotion was pleasing to Our Lady and that she desired it to be propagated.[77]

Asked whether she thought that the scapular was "part of the Fatima message," Lucia replied, "Most definitely, the scapular and the Rosary are inseparable. The scapular is a sign of consecration to Our Lady."[78]

Lucia was even stronger in speaking with Carmelite Father Howard Rafferty on the feast of the Assumption in 1950, when he noted that books so far did not list the scapular as a necessary part of the Fatima message. He made it very clear: "Lucia said immediately, 'Oh, they are wrong; Our Lady wants all to wear the scapular.'"[79]

---

[76] John Haffert, *Her Glorious Title: Our Lady of Mount Carmel — Star of the Sea* (Asbury, NJ: 101 Foundation, 1993), 29.

[77] Lynch, *Our Lady of Fatima and the Brown Scapular*, 15.

[78] Ibid.

[79] Ibid., 15–16.

The priest asked if Mary wanted the scapular as part of the Message. Lucia said, "Yes." And she added, "Now the Holy Father has already told this to the whole world, saying that the scapular is a sign of consecration to the Immaculate Heart. Nobody can disagree now."

Another time, she repeated that at Fatima Our Lady of Mount Carmel held and showed the brown scapular "Because She wants everyone to wear it. As Pope Pius XII has said, 'It is the sign of consecration to Her Immaculate Heart.'" [80]

Father Rafferty persisted: Was the scapular also a condition of the Fatima message? "Yes, certainly," Lucia answered. "Yes, the Rosary and the scapular are inseparable."

How can we not say that the scapular constantly reminds us of the "need of prayer," of the daily Rosary that our Blessed Mother asked for at Fatima, and for consecration to her Immaculate Heart?

The Vision of Our Lady of Sorrows

In the final October 13 Fatima apparition, Mary identified herself as Our Lady of the Rosary. This confirmed her request, during each apparition, for us to pray the Rosary daily.

Next, she appeared as Our Lady of Mount Carmel. Finally, she appeared under another of her major titles — Our Lady of Sorrows. If our Blessed Mother appeared as Our Lady of the Rosary to give us a message about the necessity of praying the Rosary, and she appeared as Our Lady of Mount Carmel to give us a message about wearing the brown scapular, then she must have appeared as Our Lady of Sorrows to give us another message.

[80] Haffert, *Her Glorious Title*, 29, 72, 113.

In her book *"Calls" from the Message of Fatima,* Sister Lucia sheds light on the connection of this title to Fatima: "Mary, made one with Christ, is the co-redemptrix of the human race."[81]

Lucia explains how, at Calvary, Mary "suffered and agonized with Him, receiving into her Immaculate Heart the last sufferings of Christ, His last words, His last agony, and the last drops of His Blood, in order to offer them to the Father."[82]

Interpreting this vision of Our Lady of Sorrows, Lucia adds that God wishes "to show us the value of suffering, sacrifice, and immolation for the sake of love. In the world of today hardly anyone wants to hear these truths, such is the extent to which people are living in search of pleasure, of empty worldly happiness, and exaggerated comfort. But the more one flees from suffering, the more we find ourselves immersed in a sea of afflictions, disappointments, and suffering."[83]

How can we console our Blessed Mother, Our Lady of Sorrows? Again, Fatima has the answers.

One way was revealed during the July 13 apparition, when Our Lady told the children, "Make sacrifices for sinners, and say often, especially while making a sacrifice, 'O Jesus, this is for love of Thee, for the conversion of sinners, and in reparation for offenses committed against the Immaculate Heart of Mary.'" Even the smallest sacrifice can have very great merit. One of the saints said that even picking up a pin off the floor — a pin that you didn't want to pick up — is a sacrifice.[84]

---

[81] *"Calls,"* 137.

[82] Ibid.

[83] Ibid., 178.

[84] St. Thérèse of Lisieux said, "To pick up a pin can convert a soul." *Letters of Saint Thérèse, Volume II,* May 22, 1894 (Washington, D.C.: ICS Publications, 1988), 855.

The Fruits of Fatima

Another way of consoling Our Lady is to undertake the Five First Saturdays devotion. Even if you've already done the devotion once, you may continue it on every first Saturday.

Our Lady first told the children about this devotion during the July 13 apparition. She said, "I shall ask that on the first Saturday of every month, Communions of reparation be made in atonement for the sins of the world."

All the details of the Five First Saturdays devotion would later come together for us on December 10, 1925, when Our Lady and Jesus appeared to Lucia in her convent in Pontevedra, Spain. As an extra, so to speak, the date happened to be the feast of Our Lady of Loreto, which celebrates the Holy House of Nazareth, where Mary gave her *Fiat*, where Jesus was incarnated, and where He grew up with Mary and Joseph — there's a reminder of the Holy Family again.

Comforting Our Lady in her sorrows also means putting into practice what she said in each apparition, including on October 13: "I want you to continue saying the Rosary every day."

Fatima tells us that this is one of the ways we can comfort Our Lady of Sorrows. It is notable that the Rosary also plays a major part in the Five First Saturdays devotion. Another part is receiving Communion on those Saturdays. This is not surprising, because there was already a major connection between Fatima and the Holy Eucharist.

Later, we'll take a closer look at this Fatima-Eucharist connection and the reasons for, details of, and promises attached to the First Saturday devotions. Heaven weaves these several requests and devotions together so that they form a beautiful spiritual picture for us to learn how each intertwines with the other. In this case, Fatima prompts us to take a closer look at Our Lady of Sorrows.

Our Lady's Seven Sorrows and Seven Promises

Let's briefly take a closer look at Our Lady of Sorrows, since Mary appeared under this title on October 13. At times, feasts of Our Lady and of her Son, Jesus, are linked. The feast of Our Lady of Sorrows is fittingly celebrated on September 15, the day after her Son's feast, the Exaltation of the Holy Cross. The connection between these feasts begins at the Crucifixion.

Could it be that Our Lady, appearing in Fatima as Our Lady of Sorrows, was not only recommending devotion to her sorrowful heart but also leading us to several promises she and Jesus had made? As Our Lady of Sorrows, our Blessed Mother had earlier granted several promises to those who would honor her under this title, and Jesus added four more promises for this devotion.

Before we look at these promises, let's recall what the Seven Sorrows are. Here's a quick glance at where the devotion originated.

The Church has celebrated the Exaltation of the Holy Cross since 326, when St. Helen discovered Christ's True Cross on Calvary on September 14. The feast became prominent in the West in the seventh century.

In the fourth century, Ephrem the Syrian and St. Ambrose celebrated and venerated Mary's sorrows and compassion. In 1239, the sorrows of Mary standing under the Cross became the main devotion of the new order the Servants of Mary, or Servites. In 1814, the Holy See placed the feast of Our Lady of Sorrows on the Roman calendar.

These are the Seven Sorrows of Mary:

1. The prophecy of Simeon
2. The fight into Egypt
3. The loss of the Child Jesus for three days in the Temple

4. The meeting of Jesus and Mary on the Way of the Cross
5. The Crucifixion
6. The taking down of the body of Jesus from the Cross
7. The burial of Jesus

Marian expert Dr. Mark Miravalle explains, "So much does the Crucified Lord desire humanity to ponder, along with His own saving Redemption, the co-redemption of His Mother, that He has attached to the prayerful meditation of the seven principal historical events of Our Lady's sufferings promises of grace and mercy that are nothing short of extraordinary and miraculous."

Now for the promises. Our Blessed Mother revealed these seven promises to St. Bridget of Sweden in the fourteenth century. Our Lady said she would bestow seven graces on those souls who honor her daily by saying seven Hail Marys while meditating on her tears and sorrows:

1. I will grant peace to their families.
2. They will be enlightened about the divine mysteries.
3. I will console them in their pains, and I will accompany them in their work.
4. I will give them as much as they ask for, as long as it does not oppose the adorable will of my divine Son or the sanctification of their souls.
5. I will defend them in their spiritual battles with the infernal enemy, and I will protect them at every instant of their lives.
6. I will visibly help them at the moment of their death —they will see the face of their mother.
7. I have obtained this grace from my divine Son that those who propagate this devotion to my tears and

dolors will be taken directly from this earthly life to eternal happiness, since all their sins will be forgiven, and my Son will be their eternal consolation and joy.[85]

In *The Glories of Mary*, St. Alphonsus Liguori lists four promises made by Jesus to those devoted to His Mother's sorrows. St. Alphonsus recounts the revelation made to St. Elizabeth of Hungary that St. John the Evangelist wanted to see the Blessed Virgin after her Assumption into heaven:

The favor was granted him; his dear Mother appeared to him, and with her Jesus Christ also appeared; St. John then heard Mary ask her Son to grant some special grace to all those who are devoted to her dolors. Jesus promised her four principal ones:

1. Those who before death invoke the Divine Mother in the name of her sorrows should obtain true repentance of all their sins.

2. He will protect all who have this devotion in their tribulations, and He will protect them especially at the hour of death.

3. He will impress upon their minds the remembrance of His Passion, and they will have their reward for it in heaven.

4. He will commit such devout clients to the hands of Mary, with the power to dispose of them in whatever manner she might please and to obtain for them all the graces she might desire.[86]

---

85 "Devotion to Our Lady of Sorrows," Our Sorrowful Mothers Ministry, www.osmm.org/devotion/devotion-our-lady-sorrows.

86 St. Alphonsus Ligouri, *The Glories of Mary* (New York: P. J. Kenedy and Sons, 1888), 534.

The Fruits of Fatima

It seems that we can surely call this another bonus of the Fatima apparitions. We can't measure the love and generosity that our Blessed Mother and her Son pour out on us. As we meditate on the Rosary on first Saturdays, it would be beneficial to focus especially on the Sorrowful Mysteries sometimes, remembering this vision. We could even focus on the fourth and fifth mysteries — the Carrying of the Cross and the Crucifixion — and Mary's role during the Passion and Death of her Son.

St. Alphonsus also presents the insights of major saints who saw the connection between Our Lady of Sorrows and her crucified Son. A look at just one of them helps us visualize Our Lady's sorrows and our need to take them to heart, to console and honor her.

Our Lady told St. Bridget that even after Jesus' Ascension into heaven, whether she was working or eating, the memory of His Passion was deeply imprinted and always in her tender heart.

An angel also addressed these words to St. Bridget: "As the rose grows up amongst thorns, so the Mother of God advanced in years in the midst of sufferings; and as the thorns increase with the growth of the rose, so also did the thorns of her sorrows increase in Mary, the chosen rose of the Lord, as she advanced in age; and so much the more deeply did they pierce her heart."[87]

St. Alphonsus says that the angel also told her that this Mother was so merciful and kind that she was "willing to suffer any pain, rather than to see souls unredeemed or left in their former perdition. It may be said that this was the only consolation of Mary in the midst of her great sorrow at the Passion of her Son, to see the lost world redeemed by His death, and men,

---

[87] St. Alphonsus Liguori, "Of the Dolours of Mary," EWTN, www.ewtn.com/library/MARY/7DOLORS.htm.

who were His enemies, reconciled with God."[88] And didn't Our Lady come to Fatima to show us the road to her Son and heaven? As Our Lady of Sorrows at Fatima, she was surely asking us to console her in her sorrows by turning to Jesus and by listening to her counsel on the specific ways to do that. But did people listen in great numbers?

Back to St. Bridget's vision:

> But of this [Mary] complained to St. Bridget, that very few pitied her, and most lived forgetful of her sorrows: "I look around upon all who are in the world, if perchance there may be any to pity me and meditate upon my sorrows, and truly I find very few. Therefore, my daughter, though I am forgotten by many, at least do not thou forget me; behold my anguish, and imitate, as far as thou canst, my grief."[89]

At Fatima, she was asking us not to forget her as Our Lady of Sorrows. Why? During the October 13 apparition, Our Lady told the children, "People must amend their lives and ask pardon for their sins. They must not offend our Lord anymore, for He is already too much offended!"

To offend our Lord is to hurt Our Lady, too, because, as at Calvary, to see Him hurt and offended so causes her to suffer the most. As Fatima tells us, people must stop offending Jesus our Lord, and that, in turn, will comfort Our Lady, His Mother.

Will we finally listen and do both?

---

88   Ibid.
89   St. Alphonsus Ligouri, *The Glories of Mary*, 532–533.

3

St. Joseph Appears at Fatima

St. Joseph, the model of fatherhood, is also part of the Fatima apparitions. When the one hundredth anniversary of Fatima was celebrated in 2017, many people renewed their acquaintance with the Miracle of the Sun, and many others may have heard about it for the first time. But few realize that during the October 1917 apparition, St. Joseph also appeared.

Lucia described this blessed appearance in her memoirs: "After Our Lady had disappeared into the immense distance of the firmament, we beheld St. Joseph with the Child Jesus and Our Lady robed in white with a blue mantle, beside the sun. St. Joseph and the Child Jesus seemed to bless the world, for they traced the Sign of the Cross with their hands."[90]

The Holy Family's presence at the last Fatima apparition is a timely reminder for today's families and a timely reminder of the importance of St. Joseph himself. We forget St. Joseph too often, but we should correct that. Fatima is a reminder to call on him frequently — daily, in fact. After all, he is the foster father of Jesus, the head of the Holy Family. His name appears in

---

[90] *Memoirs*, 183.

the Canon of the Mass, and, after our Blessed Mother, he is the greatest of all saints and angels.

Among its other meanings, Fatima is a reminder of the importance of fatherhood. "The fatherhood of St. Joseph, as with all human fathers, is a reflection in a creature of the fatherhood of God the Father," emphasized Monsignor Joseph Cirrincione in his booklet *St. Joseph, Fatima and Fatherhood*.[91] "The vision of St. Joseph and the Infant Jesus blessing the world, with Mary by the side of the sun, which has *not* left its place, is God's assurance that although man may reject Him, God will never reject man."[92]

When the peaceful scene is disrupted by the sun's gyrations during the Miracle of the Sun, Monsignor Cirrincione sees "an ominous foreshadowing of the consequences for the world, which are sure to be felt if the true fatherhood of God and the traditional strong role of the father of the family are rejected by mankind."

He adds, "The Miracle of the Sun represents not so much a threat of evils to come as it does a foreshadowing of the dethronement of God the Father and an intimation of the appalling consequences to follow."[93]

All we need to do is look at the attacks on fatherhood and the family during the latter half of the twentieth century, which increased as we entered the twenty-first century. St. Joseph appearing at Fatima was surely a warning about what might happen if we didn't heed the messages of Fatima.

---

[91] Msgr. Joseph Cirrincione, *St. Joseph, Fatima and Fatherhood* (Rockford, IL: TAN Books, 1989), 9.

[92] Ibid., 43.

[93] Ibid., 8.

Monsignor Cirrincione explains, "Since human fatherhood, as a reflection of the fatherhood of God, was designed to be the pillar of the family, the disappearance of esteem for fatherhood has led to the collapse of that pillar and to the disintegration of the family."[94]

St. Joseph's appearance at Fatima during the final apparition is yet another heavenly message about his importance in this respect and in other respects as well.

St. Joseph may not have used words during his appearance, but as head of the Holy Family, his silence speaks eloquently about the company we keep.

Let's ask ourselves: Whom did he spend time with every day? Whom did he live with? Whom did he talk to and listen to? The answer is simple and clear: Mary and Jesus.

What a lesson St. Joseph gives to fathers, and what a model he provides for them as a foundation for leading their families! In fact, what a lesson it is for every member of the family!

Fathers today—and this goes for father figures too—need to spend time with Jesus and Mary every day, modeling themselves after St. Joseph. He shows the way. Daily Mass, Scripture reading, and quiet prayer are all good ways to spend quality time with Jesus and Mary.

Speaking of St. Joseph, Pope Francis said:

Joseph was for Jesus the example and the teacher of the wisdom that is nourished by the Word of God. We could ponder how Joseph formed the little Jesus to listen to the Sacred Scriptures, above all by accompanying him on Saturday to the Synagogue in Nazareth. Joseph accompanied

---

[94] Ibid., 40.

Jesus so that he would listen to the Word of God in the Synagogue.... St Joseph is the model of the educator and the dad, the father.[95]

The father, layman, or priest who models St. Joseph by spending time visibly every day with Jesus and Mary will, by silent example, bring his family closer to the Holy Family. At home, the domestic church will become a stronghold, a fortress, built on the most solid of foundations that nothing will shake.

Simple, ordinary life presents constant occasions for holiness in daily tasks. John Paul II affirmed this reality in *Redemptoris Custos*: "St. Joseph ... is the proof that in order to be a good and genuine follower of Christ ... it is enough to have the common, simple, and human virtues, but they need to be true and authentic." Keep this in mind later when we discuss sacrifice.

If the Rosary had been around two thousand years ago, surely St. Joseph would have prayed it daily. After all, wasn't it eventually given to us by his wife? And at Fatima, did she not ask us to pray it daily? And doesn't a loving husband want to please his wife in all things good, especially for eternal salvation of souls?

Didn't St. Joseph live the Joyful Mysteries daily with Jesus and Mary? It's time to do what the Bible says: *Ite ad Joseph*—"go to Joseph" (Gen. 41:55)—and follow his lead.

Speaking of St. Joseph, the Rosary, and Fatima, years before the apparitions and before anyone knew of Fatima, there was already a foreshadowing of the events to come. Pope Leo XIII, in his 1883 encyclical *Supremi Apostolatus Officio*, consecrated

[95] Francis, General Audience, March 19, 2014.

October to Our Lady of the Rosary—the title Mary would use to identify herself at Fatima during the October apparition. And in his 1889 encyclical *Quamquam Pluries*, Pope Leo asked "for the Christian people continually to invoke, with great piety and trust, together with the Virgin Mother of God, her chaste Spouse, the Blessed Joseph."[96]

Because of the "high importance," of devotion to St. Joseph in the daily practices of Catholics, Pope Leo provided a prayer to St. Joseph to be recited after the Rosary during October:

> To thee, O blessed Joseph, we have recourse in our afflic-tion, and having implored the help of your thrice-holy Spouse, we now, with hearts filled with confidence, ear-nestly beg you also to take us under your protection. By that charity wherewith you were united to the Immacu-late Virgin Mother of God, and by that fatherly love with which you cherished the Child Jesus, we beseech you and we humbly pray that you will look down with gracious eye upon that inheritance which Jesus Christ purchased by His blood, and will succor us in our need by your power and strength.
>
> Defend, O most watchful guardian of the Holy Family, the chosen offspring of Jesus Christ. Keep from us, O most loving father, all blight of error and corruption. Aid us from on high, most valiant defender, in this conflict with the powers of darkness. And even as of old you rescued the Child Jesus from the peril of His life, so now defend God's Holy Church from the snares of the enemy and from all adversity. Shield us ever under your patronage,

---

[96] Leo XIII, Encyclical *Quamquam Pluries* (August 15, 1889), no. 2.

that, following your example and strengthened by your help, we may live a holy life, die a happy death, and attain to everlasting bliss in Heaven. Amen.

Keeping the holy example of St. Joseph in mind is a key part of Catholic devotion. As Pope Leo wrote, "The Blessed Patriarch looks upon the multitude of Christians who make up the Church as confided specially to his trust—this limitless family spread over the earth, over which, because he is the spouse of Mary and the father of Jesus Christ, he holds, as it were, a paternal authority."[97]

And less than thirty years later, St. Joseph would appear at Fatima together with the Child Jesus, blessing the world and it's "limitless family spread over the earth."

Pope Leo wrote also, "It is, then, natural and worthy that as the Blessed Joseph ministered to all the needs of the family at Nazareth and girt it about with his protection, he should now cover with the cloak of his heavenly patronage and defend the Church of Jesus Christ."

Further, one of the greatest benefits connected with the scapular is that "being special children of Mary the scapular-wearers are all special children of St. Joseph, her spouse," according to John Haffert.[98] If one parent adopts a child, certainly the spouse does the same. As we are children of Mary, so we're also adopted by her spouse, Joseph. If she is Mother of the scapular family, he is the father of the scapular family. They clothe us their children, feed us, and educate us with virtue. Haffert goes so far as to say that we become "a family of predestined ones" that anyone can become a part of. "Anyone may join them and enjoy the special

---

[97] Ibid., no. 3.
[98] John Haffert, *Mary in Her Scapular Promise*, 2nd ed. (Sea Isle, NJ: Scapular Press, 1942), 148.

love of those parents whom God molded to the greatest possible perfection. Such is the significance of Mary and Joseph in the Scapular."[99] With these heavenly parents of our Blessed Mother and St. Joseph, how can we help but stay safely on the right, narrow path heavenward?

Now that we know these details and forgotten Fatima facts, we should be running to listen to Our Lady and to get enrolled in the brown scapular[100] to wear it as her uniform — especially knowing that we have St. Joseph there as a silent part of the scapular devotion.

St. Joseph has been neglected for too long. Fatima reminds us of this fact, shows us his boundless importance, and urges us on to go to St. Joseph and to honor him.

---

[99] Ibid., 152.

[100] Enrollment in the brown scapular is a simple ceremony that any priest can perform.

4

Fatima and Eucharistic Devotion

Our Lady of Fatima leads us to discover the connections between Our Lady of the Rosary, Our Lady of Mount Carmel, and Our Lady of Sorrows. Because Mary always brings us to Jesus, there is yet another connection she made for us—her connection to the Blessed Sacrament. That connection was clear from the very beginning and continued beyond 1917, when Jesus and Mary appeared to Lucia in her convent and spoke again about the Five First Saturdays devotion, which includes receiving Holy Communion as one of the requirements. More on this later. Right now, let's go back to the first apparition at Fatima on May 13.

When Our Lady of Fatima first appeared in 1917, in addition to her consistent theme and constant calls to pray the Rosary every day, she included vital lessons on the Blessed Sacrament.

Because heaven doesn't act coincidentally but presents everything meaningfully to us, surely there is a providential reason that the date of Our Lady's first apparition—May 13—was also celebrated in some parts of the Church as the feast of Our Lady of the Blessed Sacrament. The children intuitively realized the connection, maybe not because they recognized the celebration on that date, but based on what happened during the apparition. Let's take a closer look.

Much later, describing that appearance in 1917, Lucia would write that Our Lady opened her hands, and from them streamed light "so intense" that it penetrated their "hearts and innermost depths of our souls."[101]

Realizing it was God "who was that light," Lucia fell to her knees. So did her cousins Jacinta and Francisco. As Lucia recalls in her memoirs, the trio then began to pray, "O most Holy Trinity, I adore You! My God, my God, I love You in the most Blessed Sacrament!"[102]

It was a variation of the prayer the children had learned during the third visit of the Angel of Peace, who appeared to them in 1916 to prepare these little shepherds for Our Lady's appearance the following year. The Holy Eucharist was a major part of the preparation. In his left hand, the angel held a chalice with a Host suspended in the air over it. Drops of blood fell from the Host into the chalice.

The angel left the chalice and the Host suspended in the air, knelt, and told the children to repeat three times:

> Most Holy Trinity, Father, Son, and Holy Spirit, I adore You profoundly, and I offer You the most precious Body, Blood, Soul, and Divinity of Jesus Christ, present in all the tabernacles of the world, in reparation for the outrages, sacrileges, and indifferences by which He Himself is offended. And, through the infinite merits of His most Sacred Heart, and the Immaculate Heart of Mary, I beg of You the conversion of poor sinners.[103]

---

[101] *Memoirs*, 175.
[102] Ibid., 176.
[103] Ibid., 79.

Already the groundwork was being laid, connecting Jesus in the Eucharist to what His Mother was going to teach at Fatima. But that was not all. The angel said, "Eat and drink the Body and Blood of Jesus Christ terribly outraged by the ingratitude of men. Make reparation for their crimes and console your God." Then he rose and gave Lucia the Host and Jacinta and Francisco the Precious Blood from the chalice. As he did so, he said, "Take and drink the Body and Blood of Jesus Christ, horribly outraged by ungrateful men. Make reparation for their crimes and console your God."[104]

The following year, during Our Lady's July 13 apparition, she mentioned the First Five Saturdays devotion, the two major pillars of which are the Communion of reparation and the Rosary. Also, in the second part of the Second Secret,[105] she said, "To prevent this [World War II and the persecution of the Church and the Holy Father], I shall come to the world to ask that Russia be consecrated to my Immaculate Heart, and I shall ask that, on the first Saturday of every month, Communions of reparation be made in atonement for the sins of the world."

If that was the situation in 1916–1917, how much more is such a devotion needed today? Through the seers, Our Lady was teaching us, her children, that our devotion to the Blessed Sacrament must increase. And we have to receive the Eucharist worthily. Confession is also one of the requirements of the First Saturdays devotion.[106] This was woven into the beautiful pattern

---

[104] Ibid.

[105] In her July 13 apparition, Our Lady revealed a prophetic Secret to the three seers. The three parts of the Secret are sometimes referred to as the First, Second, and Third Secrets, and sometimes as the first, second, and third parts of the Secret.

[106] Our Lady said, "I promise to assist at the hour of death, with the graces necessary for salvation, all those who, on the first

at the October 13 apparition when Our Lady told the children, "People must amend their lives and ask pardon for their sins. They must not offend our Lord any more, for He is already too much offended!"

The first step in amending our lives is to receive the sacrament of Confession and get rid of our sins. And what do we normally do after Confession but go to Mass and receive Holy Communion. Yet so often we forget these major lessons of Fatima and slip up on putting them into practice.

Let's hear from another source on this connection of Our Lady of Fatima to the Most Blessed Sacrament. Father Bernard Camire of the Congregation of the Blessed Sacrament draws the connection between Our Lady and the Eucharist in his booklet *The Eucharist and St. Peter Julian Eymard*. His community's founder was St. Peter Julian Eymard, who "taught that, at the level of the sacramental life of the Church, Mary helps us to perceive the central place of the Eucharist in our personal life and in the life of the Church."[107]

Providentially, it was St. Peter Julian Eymard who was first to give Mary the title "Our Lady of the Blessed Sacrament," in May 1868. This saint, who had a strong devotion to the Holy Eucharist and to Our Lady, founded the Congregation of the Most

---

Saturday of five consecutive months, shall confess, receive Holy Communion, recite five decades of the Rosary, and keep me company for fifteen minutes while meditating on the fifteen mysteries of the Rosary, with the intention of making reparation to me." See chapter 6 for more on the First Five Saturdays devotion.

[107] Fr. Bernard Camire, *The Eucharist and Saint Peter Julian Eymard* (Cleveland: Emmanuel Publishing, 2011), 41.

Blessed Sacrament on May 13, 1856, and they celebrate the feast of Our Lady of the Blessed Sacrament on May 13.

Jump ahead a century plus a few decades, and Pope John Paul II, who undoubtedly had a major connection with Fatima and credited Our Lady of Fatima with saving his life, wrote in *Ecclesia de Eucharistia*, "Mary is a 'woman of the Eucharist' in her whole life. The Church, which looks to Mary as a model, is also called to imitate her in her relationship with this most holy mystery."[108]

He observed, "If the Church and the Eucharist are inseparably united, the same ought to be said of Mary and the Eucharist.... Mary is present ... at each of our celebrations of the Eucharist."[109] Just stop and think of that for a moment. Every time we're at Mass, our Blessed Mother is right there with us.

A few years after John Paul II published that encyclical letter, Pope Benedict XVI in his 2008 Message for the World Day of the Sick said, "There is an indissoluble link between the Mother and the Son, generated in her womb by work of the Holy Spirit, and this link we perceive, in a mysterious way, in the sacrament of the Eucharist."[110] There it is again. Read that line over, and put it together with Our Lady of Fatima and what she was telling us in 1917.

There is another link we so often forget, yet that is essential in all of these connections. "Except for Our Lady, we would not have the Holy Eucharist. It was only because she became the Virgin Mother of the Son of God that we have the Holy Eucharist," explained Servant of God Father John Hardon. "The Eucharist

---

[108] John Paul II, Encyclical Letter *Ecclesia de Eucharistia* (April 17, 2003), no. 53.

[109] Ibid., no. 57.

[110] Benedict XVI, Message for the Sixteenth World Day of the Sick (January 11, 2008), no. 2.

is the living Jesus Christ.... It is because Mary gave her Son his body and blood that we now have the Eucharist."[111]

Ninety years earlier, the three Fatima seers came to realize the connection and became models of devotion to the Blessed Sacrament. During his final illness, Francisco said what hurt him most was that he couldn't go to the church "and stay awhile with the Hidden Jesus."[112] It was his favorite name for Jesus in the Eucharist, hidden in the tabernacle. Francisco, who received and lived the requests of Our Lady of Fatima, had become very devoted to the Blessed Sacrament, spending hours on end before the tabernacle to console the Hidden Jesus.

He teaches us something of significant importance connected with Fatima through his love for the Blessed Sacrament and the time he spent before the Hidden Jesus. As Father Frederick Miller observes, "Obviously, the practice of Eucharistic reparation is another component of the Fatima catechesis and an important lesson for our time."[113]

In 1919, at age eleven, Francisco died at home peacefully, despite suffering terribly from the influenza epidemic of 1918. His greatest wish, to receive Jesus in the Holy Eucharist, was granted the day before he died. Although he had received from the chalice that the angel offered him in 1916 before Our Lady appeared the following year, this was his First Holy Communion. With his devotion to the Hidden Jesus in the Blessed Sacrament,

---

[111] Fr. John A. Hardon, S.J., "An Interview: Jesuit Theologian and Author," *Soul* 42, no. 5 (September–October 1991): 11, Real Presence Association, www.therealpresence.org/archives/Mariology/Mariology_040.htm.

[112] *Memoirs*, 157.

[113] Fr. Frederick Miller, "Mary: Catechist at Fatima," 1991, EWTN, www.ewtn.com/library/MARY/CATATFAT.HTM.

and having died on the day after he received his First Holy Communion, Francisco might be thought of as a saint of the Eucharist.

As for Lucia, about four years before the apparitions of the angel, she had already received her First Holy Communion. Her parish priest had given permission because the six-year-old Lucia already had a profound ability to express the doctrine of Christ's Real Presence in the Eucharist.

Jacinta, like her brother, also used the affectionate name "Hidden Jesus" at times. When she was very ill, Lucia brought her a picture of the Blessed Sacrament. "It is the Hidden Jesus," Jacinta exclaimed. "I love Him so much. If only I could receive Him in church. Don't they receive Holy Communion in heaven? If they do, then I will go to Holy Communion every day. If only the angel would go to the hospital to bring me Holy Communion again, how happy I would be."[114]

Lucia also recorded these words of St. Jacinta: "I am so grieved to be unable to receive Communion in reparation for the sins committed against the Immaculate Heart of Mary."[115] We should all take a lesson from Jacinta and frequently offer up our Communions in reparation for sins committed against the Immaculate Heart of Mary. Think of the connection between Our Lady and the Eucharist in this way, too. If someone treated your mother kindly and wanted to make up for some hurt she had suffered, wouldn't you be overjoyed? And wouldn't Jesus' reaction be magnified beyond that more times than we can realize?

---

[114] *Memoirs*, 133.
[115] Ibid., 128.

5

The Significance of the
Immaculate Heart of Mary

We may already have a devotion to the Immaculate Heart of Mary, but maybe we don't realize the strong connection of this devotion to Fatima. Let's see how both fit together and what Our Lady is teaching us. As we learn from her, the next step for us is to put her teachings into practice for our good and the good of the world.

The June 13, 1917, apparition marked the first time Our Lady spoke about her Immaculate Heart, and she also had something to say directly to Lucia. She made it clear that ten-year-old Lucia would have to stay on earth longer. "Jesus wishes you to make me known and loved on earth," Mary told her. "He wishes also for you to establish devotion in the world to my Immaculate Heart."

When Lucia asked if she was to remain in the world alone, our Blessed Mother consoled her, saying, "I will be with you always, and my Immaculate Heart will be your comfort and the way which will lead you to God."

So far, we see that it is Jesus, Mary's Son, who wants to make her known and loved, with devotion established in the world to her Immaculate Heart. And the Immaculate Heart will be not only our comfort but the way that will lead us to God. Wow! It couldn't be clearer than that—reason enough why we should be devoted to the Immaculate Heart.

Recounting that June apparition, Lucia gave this description of the scene:

> The moment she said the last words, opening her hands, she transmitted to us, for the second time, the reflection of that intense light. In it we felt we were submerged in God. Jacinta and Francisco seemed to be in that part of the light which was rising to heaven, and I in the part spreading over the earth. In front of the palm of Our Lady's right hand was a heart encircled with thorns which appeared to pierce it. We understood it was the Immaculate Heart of Mary, offended by the sins of mankind, craving reparation.[116]

Right there, Lucia hinted at why our Blessed Mother would later ask for the reparation to her Immaculate Heart by instituting the Five First Saturdays devotion.

The following month, during the July 13 apparition, Our Lady told the children in detail about her Immaculate Heart, the reparation that heaven asked for, and what would happen if people ignored this request. Another hint came during the October 13 apparition, when Our Lady appeared as Our Lady of Sorrows. She again made it perfectly clear eight years later when she appeared to Lucia.

Notice the specific reference to her heart that Our Lady gave the children in this short prayer: "Make sacrifices for sinners, and say often, especially while making a sacrifice: O Jesus, this is for

---

[116] "100 Years of Fatima."

love of Thee, for the conversion of sinners, and in reparation for offenses committed against the Immaculate Heart of Mary."

Let's remind ourselves who it was that asked for this devotion: her Son, Jesus.

Then, in the July 13 apparition, after Our Lady had shown the children a vision of hell, where poor sinners go, she told them, "It is to save them that God wants to establish in the world devotion to my Immaculate Heart. If you do what I tell you, many souls will be saved, and there will be peace."

During the same apparition, Our Lady referred twice more to her Immaculate Heart when she called for the consecration of Russia and the Five First Saturdays devotion. Our Blessed Mother didn't give the details of the Five First Saturdays devotion yet. That was to come later. But she made clear what would happen concerning the devotion to her Immaculate Heart: "If my wishes are fulfilled, Russia will be converted, and there will be peace; if not, then Russia will spread her errors throughout the world, bringing new wars and persecution of the Church; the good will be martyred, and the Holy Father will have much to suffer; certain nations will be annihilated. But in the end my Immaculate Heart will triumph."

The triumph will come through her Immaculate Heart. Nothing and no one will prevent this. We just have to make sure we're helping Our Lady by living out her requests because heaven wants our cooperation and devotion.

Later, apparitions to Sister Lucia continued this same theme. The major one on December 10, 1925, when Our Lady appeared to her in the convent in Pontevedra, Spain, bears repeating because it needs to be fulfilled today more urgently than ever.

Lucia would describe the visit, saying, her "dear Mother" came with the Child Jesus standing on a luminous cloud by her side.

"Our Lady, as if wanting to instill courage, rested her hand on my shoulder, and as she did so, she showed me her Immaculate Heart encircled by thorns, which she was holding in her other hand. The Child Jesus said, 'Have compassion on the Heart of your Most Holy Mother, covered with thorns, with which ungrateful men pierce it at every moment, and there is no one to make an act of reparation to remove them.'"[117]

Then the Blessed Virgin Mary said to Lucia:

> Look, my daughter, at my Heart, surrounded with thorns with which ungrateful men pierce me at every moment by their blasphemies and ingratitude. You at least try to console me and say that I promise to assist at the hour of death, with the graces necessary for salvation, all those who, on the first Saturday of five consecutive months, shall confess, receive Holy Communion, recite five decades of the Rosary, and keep me company for fifteen minutes while meditating on the fifteen mysteries of the Rosary, with the intention of making reparation to me.[118]

Lucia continued to receive visions reinforcing the importance of devotion to the Immaculate Heart. On February 15, 1926, the Child Jesus appeared to Lucia and asked, "And have you spread through the world what our heavenly Mother requested of you?"[119]

Then, three years later, on June 6, 1929, at the convent in Tuy, Spain, another major supernatural event happened—Lucia saw a vision of the Holy Trinity. Jesus appeared crucified, and, from the wound in His side, drops ran down upon a Host and

---

[117] Carmel of Coimbra, A Pathway, 158.

[118] Ibid.

[119] Ibid., 160.

fell into a chalice below. Lucia writes, "Beneath the right arm of the Cross was Our Lady, and in her hand was *her Immaculate Heart*. (It was Our Lady of Fatima, with her Immaculate Heart in her left hand, without sword or roses, but with a crown of thorns and flames)."[120]

What our Blessed Mother requested during this apparition ties in to the July 13, 1917, apparition. At the same time, the connection between Fatima and the Eucharist again appeared during this vision, which contained a Host and a chalice with Jesus' blood falling into it.

Now let's look at the Five First Saturdays devotion that Our Lady of Fatima requested.

---

[120] *Memoirs*, 197.

6

The Essential Five First Saturdays Devotion

With regular Sunday Mass attendance dropping off in recent years, how many people, even those who have heard of Fatima and Our Lady's requests, are carrying out the Five First Saturdays devotion? It must surely be necessary for us to listen to Our Mother's instructions to pray a daily Rosary and honor the Five First Saturdays. Indeed, how could we pass up on receiving the great promise Our Lady gave for everyone who heeded her call to this devotion?

She gave each of us this promise when, in 1925, she appeared with the Christ Child to Sister Lucia, then a postulant at a convent in Spain. Although we've just considered that vision, the words of Jesus and our Blessed Mother bear repeating.

Jesus spoke first, saying, "Have compassion on the Heart of your Most Holy Mother which is covered with thorns that most ungrateful men drive into it every instant, while there is no one who does an act of reparation to withdraw them from her."[121]

Then the Blessed Mother spoke:

Look, my daughter, at my Heart, surrounded with thorns with which ungrateful men pierce me at every moment

---

[121] Carmel of Coimbra, A Pathway, 158.

by their blasphemies and ingratitude. You at least try to console me and say that I promise to assist at the hour of death, with the graces necessary for salvation, all those who, on the first Saturday of five consecutive months, shall confess, receive Holy Communion, recite five decades of the Rosary, and keep me company for fifteen minutes while meditating on the fifteen mysteries of the Rosary, with the intention of making reparation to me.[122]

Fatima expert Father Andrew Apostoli, one of the co-founders of the Franciscan Friars of the Renewal, strongly stated in an interview, "This devotion is most important and neglected. I call it Our Lady's spiritual formation program. It's one of the most important elements for the peace of the world and the consecration and conversion of Russia. With Russia, the pope did his part. What's not happened is we're not making the Five First Saturdays devotion in numbers sufficient."[123]

Father Apostoli also said in his book *Fatima for Today*, "As a mother, Our Lady wants none of her children to be lost, but all to be saved. So let us faithfully and generously carry out her wishes in this great devotion of the Five First Saturdays. The Five First Saturdays devotion, with its unique combination of confession, Communion, and the Rosary, holds a special place in Our Lady's plan."[124]

---

[122] Ibid.

[123] Joseph Pronechen, "Listen to Your Mother!" *National Catholic Register*, May 14, 2014, www.ncregister.com/blog/joseph-pronechen/listen-to-your-mother1.

[124] Fr. Andrew Apostoli, C.F.R., *Fatima for Today: The Urgent Marian Message of Hope* (San Francisco: Ignatius Press, 2010), 247–248.

The Five First Saturdays devotion, which Our Lady also called the "Communion of reparation," carries with it that exciting promise from Our Lady for the individual as well as for the world. That's right. Our Lady herself assures that those who make this devotion will receive from her the graces necessary for salvation at the moment of their death.

On May 29, 1930, Jesus appeared to Sister Lucia again and explained the reasons for this reparation to Our Lady—and why it is five Saturdays. He said, "My daughter, the motive is simple: there are five ways in which people offend and blaspheme against the Immaculate Heart of Mary."[125]

Jesus listed the blasphemies:

1. Against her Immaculate Conception
2. Against her perpetual virginity
3. Against her divine maternity, refusing also to accept her as the mother of all mankind
4. By those trying publicly to implant in children's hearts indifference, disrespect, contempt, and even hate against our Immaculate Mother
5. By those insulting her directly in rejecting and dishonoring her sacred images[126]

In the proverbial nutshell, here's how to observe the Five First Saturdays. Do the following on the first Saturday of five *consecutive* months:

1. Go to Confession within eight days before or after the first Saturday of the month.[127]

---

[125] Ibid., 157.

[126] Martins, *Documents on Fatima*, 284.

[127] When the Child Jesus visited Sister Lucia on February 15, 1926, Lucia asked about those who found it difficult to go to Confession on the first Saturday. She asked if it would be okay for them

2. Receive Holy Communion on the first Saturday of the month.
3. Recite five decades of the Rosary.
4. Meditate on the mysteries of the Rosary for fifteen minutes, keeping Mary company. Remember one or more mysteries with the intention of making reparation to her Immaculate Heart.

Remember to do this with the intention of making reparation to the Immaculate Heart of Mary.

So as to make the First Saturdays with dedication and enthusiasm, keep in mind something else Jesus told Sister Lucia when He appeared to her on February 15:

> It is true, my daughter, that many souls begin the first Saturdays, but few finish them, and those who do complete them do so in order to receive the graces that are promised thereby. It would please me more if they did five with fervor and with the intention of making reparation to the Heart of your heavenly Mother, than if they did fifteen, in a tepid and indifferent manner.[128]

Don't postpone, put off, or procrastinate starting the First Saturdays devotion. If it seems like an inconvenience at first, don't let that be an excuse. Decide and determine to carry it out. You'll find after the first one that each successive Saturday becomes easier. And you will look forward to it. It gives great

to go to confession within eight days of that first Saturday. Our Lord responded, "Yes, and it can be longer provided that when they receive Me on the first Saturday they are in the state of grace and have the intention of making reparation to the Immaculate Heart of Mary." Carmel of Coimbra, A *Pathway*, 161.

[128] *Memoirs*, 196.

joy as you complete them to know that you are doing your part in comforting Our Lady and making reparations for the sins committed against her Immaculate Heart, as she and her Son requested. (Wouldn't you want to comfort your mother if anyone insulted her?) And you will find that, after the first five, you will want to continue them month after month for these reasons.

Another reason is to keep the second of the two great commandments: love of neighbor. The World Apostolate of Fatima describes how, after we obtain the promise for ourselves, we should continue the First Saturday devotions and "practice it all of our lives for the sake of the souls of our neighbors as well as our own. Our Lady told us that souls are being lost to hell because there is no one to make reparation for their sins. She implores us on their behalf. How can we deny her?"[129]

Along with the main purpose of this devotion, the effort to work with Our Lady for peace and to receive a personal promise of grace for salvation is a deal too good to pass up.

Why Consecration?

We've talked quite a bit about the need for consecration to our Blessed Mother, to the Immaculate Heart of Mary. So why consecration? What makes it not just important but vital today?

The Dominican friars at the Rosary Center say:

By our consecration we promise to become dependent on Mary in all things: to offer all our prayers and oblations to God through Mary and to seek every gift from God through Mary. And we do this with the greatest

---

[129] *First Saturday Devotion* (Washington, NJ: World Apostolate of Fatima, USA), 5–6.

confidence. Since she is our mother, she knows our needs better than we; and since she is Queen of Heaven, she has immediate access to the infinite treasury of graces in the Kingdom of her Divine Son.[130]

No wonder we're advised to consecrate ourselves to the Immaculate Heart of Mary. Pope Pius XII explained that this consecration "tends essentially to union with Jesus, under the guidance of Mary."[131] Jesus chose that we go to Him through Mary. As the pontiff also said, "Both the mystery of God coming to us through Mary, and our being led to God through Mary, is a work of the Holy Spirit."[132]

If we make the consecration and honestly try to live it, what the Blessed Mother promised Lucia applies to us too: "I will never leave you; my Immaculate Heart will be your refuge and the way that will lead you to God."[133]

As she was asked to do, Sister Lucia constantly promoted consecration to the Blessed Mother. On December 2, 1940, she wrote a letter to Pope Pius XII detailing the need to consecrate "the world to the Immaculate Heart of Mary" with "special mention for Russia."

Then Lucia appealed, "Now, Most Holy Father, allow me to make one more request, which is but an ardent desire of my heart; that the feast in honor of the Immaculate Heart of Mary be extended throughout the whole world as one of the main feasts of the Holy Church."[134]

---

[130] "Consecration to the Immaculate Heart of Mary," Rosary Center and Confraternity, http://www.rosary-center.org/consecrt.htm.

[131] Ibid.

[132] Ibid.

[133] Ibid.

[134] Martins, *Documents on Fatima*, 378.

In 1942, during the twenty-fifth anniversary year of Fatima, Pius XII consecrated the world to the Immaculate Heart and extended the memorial to the entire Church. It is celebrated on the day after the solemnity of the Sacred Heart of Jesus, which is celebrated on the Friday after the second Sunday of Pentecost. Because the date of Pentecost varies from year to year, so do these two major feasts. But they are always next to each other—the Sacred Heart of Jesus on Friday, the Immaculate Heart of Mary on the next day, Saturday.

The Vatican's *Directory on Popular Piety* explains the proximity of the feasts in theological terms:

> The contiguity of both celebrations is in itself a liturgical sign of their close connection: the *mysterium* of the Heart of Jesus is projected onto and reverberates in the Heart of His Mother, who is also one of his followers and a disciple. As the Solemnity of the Sacred Heart celebrates the salvific mysteries of Christ in a synthetic manner by reducing them to their fount—the Heart of Jesus, so too the memorial of the Immaculate Heart of Mary is a celebration of the complex visceral relationship of Mary with her Son's work of salvation: from the Incarnation, to his death and resurrection, to the gift of the Holy Spirit.[135]

Put simply, where the Son is, so is the Mother, and where the Mother is, so is the Son.

Honoring the Immaculate Heart

Now that we've passed the one-hundred-year mark of Fatima, late as it is, isn't it about time we begin or increase our honor

---

[135] *Directory on Popular Piety*, no. 174.

and devotion to the Immaculate Heart of Mary? Here's how to start.

- Pray the Rosary: "In our devotion to Mary's Heart there is no more effective prayer than the Rosary, which is about the mysteries of her Son's life and hers," Servant of God Father John Hardon said. "There is no better way to obtain through Mary's intercession the help we desperately need to learn how to be loving and selfless."[136] See how perfectly this fits into the June 13, 1917, apparition and Our Lady of the Rosary's first request to pray the Rosary daily? Try to follow what she asks if you're not doing so already. At least start. And tell someone else about praying the Rosary, or maybe give someone a rosary.

- Celebrate the adjoining memorial of the Immaculate Heart of Mary and the solemnity of the Sacred Heart of Jesus.

- Make or renew your consecration to the Immaculate Heart of Mary. Use St. Louis de Montfort's method, Father Michael Gaitley's *33 Days to Morning Glory*, or other suitable consecration prayers.

- Begin the Five First Saturdays devotion, or continue the first Saturday practices if you've already completed the five. You don't have to stop at five. We all can and should do them continually because they honor Our Lady and fulfill her requests.

---

[136] Fr. John Hardon, S.J., "Immaculate Heart of Mary," Real Presence Association, www.therealpresence.org/archives/Mariology/Mariology_015.htm.

• During August, do something extra, something special, something *extra special* for Our Lady. August is the month traditionally dedicated by the Church to the Immaculate Heart of Mary. Get enrolled in the brown scapular, begin wearing a Miraculous Medal, begin praying daily the Angelus or the Memorare, or why not both? Why not all? To Jesus through Mary!

The children of Fatima knew all of the above and practiced what they learned. Our Lady's messages were always close to their hearts, such as when Jacinta was exceptionally ill and about to go the hospital. She told Lucia that she would be going to heaven in a short while. Although younger than her cousin, Jacinta directed:

> You will remain here to make known that God wishes to establish in the world devotion to the Immaculate Heart of Mary. When you are to say this, don't go and hide. Tell everybody that God grants us graces through the Immaculate Heart of Mary; that people are to ask her for them; and that the Heart of Jesus wants the Immaculate Heart of Mary to be venerated at His side. Tell them also to pray to the Immaculate Heart of Mary for peace since God has entrusted it to her. If I could only put into the hearts of all the fire that is burning within my own heart, and that makes me love the Hearts of Jesus and Mary so very much![137]

What instruction from a child not quite ten!

As for Lucia, the Immaculate Heart of Mary was ever at her side. Several decades later, after the tragic events of 9/11, Cardinal Tarcisio Bertone from the Vatican went to the Carmel in

---

[137] *Memoirs*, 132.

Coimbra to speak with Sister Lucia (the second of three times he did so). He and Sister Lucia were joined by Father Louis Kondor, the vice postulator of the causes of Francisco and Jacinta, and by the prioress of the Carmelite Convent of St. Teresa.

Lucia was asked, "What effect did the vision of 13 July have on your life before it was written down and presented to the Church?"—this vision included not only the Third Secret but also the vision of hell. She answered, "I felt safe under the protection of Our Lady, who would watch carefully over the Church and the Pope."[138]

Then Lucia added a new detail about the famous prophetic vision: "During the vision, Our Lady, shining bright, held a heart in her left hand, and in her right, a Rosary," she said.[139]

Asked what the meaning of Mary's heart in her hand was, Lucia explained, "It is a symbol of love that protects and saves. It is the Mother who sees her children suffering and suffers with them, even with those who do not love her. For she wants to save them all and not to lose any of those the Lord has entrusted to her. Her Heart is a safe refuge. The devotion to the Immaculate Heart of Mary is the means of salvation for these difficult times in the Church and in the world."[140]

Cardinal Ratzinger also reflects on the Immaculate Heart of Mary at the end of his comment on the Third Secret:

"My Immaculate Heart will triumph." What does this mean? The heart open to God, purified by contemplation

---

[138] Archbishop Tarcisio Bertone, "Meeting with Sr. Maria Lucia," L'Osservatore Romano, January 9, 2002, 7, www.ewtn.com/library/curia/cdflucia.htm.

[139] Ibid.

[140] Ibid.

of God, is stronger than guns and weapons of every kind. The fiat of Mary, the word of her heart, has changed the history of the world because it brought the Savior into the world—because, thanks to her "Yes," God could become man in our world and remains so for all time. The Evil One has power in this world, as we see and experience continually; he has power because our freedom continually lets itself be led away from God. But since God Himself took a human heart and has thus steered man's freedom towards what is good, the freedom to choose evil no longer has the last word. From that time, this is the final word: "In the world you will have trouble, but take courage, I have overcome the world" (John 16:33). The message of Fatima invites us to trust in this promise.[141]

No matter how we look at it, being devoted to the Immaculate Heart of Mary and following the Fatima path is nothing less than a hope-filled journey that leads to peace and to heaven.

[141] Joseph Cardinal Ratzinger, "Theological Commentary to the Third Part of the Secret of Fatima" (June 26, 2000), posted at Crossroads Initiative, https://www.crossroadsinitiative.com/media/articles/third-secret-fatima-joseph-cardinal-ratzinger/.

7

Three Little "Doves" at Our Lady's Feet

The shepherd children immediately took Our Lady's revelations and requests to heart, began living them, and strengthened their practice day by day. They were children listening to their Mother and obeying her.

Years later, Sister Lucia beautifully described their dedication to Our Lady. Recall the story of the doves of Bombarral — how they providentially followed the statue of Our Lady of Fatima in a huge procession all the way to the Lisbon cathedral. Their actions seemed to so many people to be otherworldly.

When Father Thomas McGlynn was sculpting the statue of Our Lady that eventually was placed high on the façade of the basilica at Fatima, he asked Sister Lucia what the physical positions of her and her two cousins had been during the apparitions. Lucia did not care about the statues of the seers, however. She advised him, "Instead of the statues of the three children, it would not be bad merely to symbolize them with the three little doves at the feet of Our Lady."[142]

Like the doves that accompanied Our Lady to Lisbon, these three seers became clothed, young as they were, with heavenly

---

[142] McGlynn, *Vision of Fatima*, 169.

wonders and spirituality. Their experiences and example show us that we can take that road to holiness as they did, following Our Lady of Fatima's counsel and guidance.

Let's begin with Jacinta Marto and her brother Francisco, the two youngest nonmartyrs ever beatified and canonized. At the time of the apparitions, Jacinta was seven years old, and Francisco was nine. When they died, Jacinta was almost ten years old and Francisco eleven. The youngsters were not surprised by their early deaths, nor was Lucia, because during the June 13 apparition, the Blessed Mother had said to Lucia, "I shall take Jacinta and Francisco soon, but you will remain a little longer, since Jesus wishes you to make me known and loved on earth. He wishes also for you to establish devotion in the world to my Immaculate Heart."

For one so young, Jacinta was incredibly spiritually advanced. For example, it appears that, at least once, she bilocated. In fact, we have exceptional evidence of this reported incident. One day, Lucia's aunt wanted to ask Lucia to pray for her prodigal son. He had left home, and no one knew where he was. Lucia recalls, "Not finding me, she asked Jacinta instead, who promised to pray for him. A few days later, he suddenly returned home, asked his parents' forgiveness, and then went to Aljustrel [their hamlet] to relate his sorry story."[143] The son said he stole from his parents and wandered around like a vagrant until he ended up in jail. He then escaped from the prison and fled to remote hills. At that point, completely lost, he knelt down and prayed.

Upon returning home, he firmly declared to his family that Jacinta had appeared to him. He insisted that he recognized her perfectly. He told how she took his hand, led him to the main

---

[143] *Memoirs*, 185.

road, and pointed out the direction he needed to take. The following morning, he took that path home.

When Lucia asked Jacinta if she had helped him, Jacinta said, "I only prayed and pleaded very much with Our Lady for him, because I felt so sorry for Aunt Vitoria."[144]

Lucia writes that "only God knows" how the vision happened.[145] Lucia was always careful about what she said and wrote, as to be always in line with the Church, so the fact that she was so convinced of the heavenly connection to this event that she decided to write about it carries quite a bit of weight.

There are also examples of Jacinta's saintliness that are more typical of a child of her age. We see one such example when she, her brother, and Lucia were kidnapped and hauled off to prison by the local administrator, the atheist Artur de Oliveira Santos, who wanted the children to miss the August 13 apparition and to force them to reveal the secrets that the Blessed Mother had entrusted to them.

When questioning produced no results, he threatened to toss them into vats of burning oil. At that instant, Jacinta reacted with an unusual combination of childlike qualities and those of a mature saint facing martyrdom.

Lucia said that seven-year-old Jacinta cried uncontrollably — but not because she was afraid of the administrator's threats of torture and the possibility of dying. Jacinta sobbed, "We are going to die without ever seeing our mothers and fathers again. None of them have come to see us. They don't care for us anymore. I want to see my mother!"[146]

---

[144] Ibid., 186.

[145] Ibid.

[146] Haffert, *Russia Will Be Converted*, 45.

Francisco comforted her and told her not to cry. Then, as Lucia relates, he reminded his sister, "The Lady told us to make sacrifices for sinners, and we can offer this sacrifice for sinners."[147] He also was ready to die rather than tell the secrets entrusted to him by Our Lady.

How did Jacinta react then? At once she put into practice the prayer Our Lady taught the children to say: "My Jesus, all this is for love of You and for sinners." Then she added, "And for the Holy Father, and in reparation for the offenses against the Immaculate Heart of Mary."[148]

That brings up another little-known or little-remembered fact about Jacinta that signals her great spiritual depth for one so young. Even before Our Lady entrusted the children with the three secrets during the July 13 apparition, Jacinta received a vision. She saw a pope. He was in a big house, burying his head in his hands. Outside, a mob was about to storm the place.

After this vision, for the rest of her life she would suffer, shedding tears as she repeated, "Oh, the poor Holy Father. Oh, we must pray for the poor Holy Father!"[149]

This was yet more proof of the depth of Jacinta's spirituality. Lucia recognized this quality in her cousin. In her memoirs, she writes how she came to think, "Jacinta was the one who received from Our Lady a greater abundance of grace and a better knowledge of God and of virtue."[150]

That abundance Jacinta received, however, was not only for herself but also for everyone who would learn about her. She lived

[147] Ibid., 46.
[148] Ibid.
[149] Ibid., 57.
[150] Memoirs, 49.

the life of a saint and fashioned an example that we can benefit from following. How often do we read or hear about the lives of saints and the lessons they teach us? Jacinta built up a storehouse of such lessons for people then and for the people of the future.

In fact, she never stopped trying to cram a lifetime of evangelization into her ten years. There was the time when Lucia was quite sad because she wasn't believed and was accused of making up everything about the apparitions. When Lucia told Jacinta, her young cousin bolstered her spirit, telling Lucia that she and Francisco were going to pray for her.

"We must never be afraid of anything!" Jacinta reminded her. "The Lady will help us always. She's such a good friend of ours!"[151]

Then Jacinta prompted Lucia to recall what Our Lady told them to do. "Did you already tell Jesus that it's for love of Him?… Then I'll tell Him." Jacinta took her cousin's hand and prayed, "O Jesus, it is for love of You, and for the conversion of sinners."[152]

There she was, encouraging her older cousin by holding firmly to the Fatima messages from Our Lady. Do we do the same?

Jacinta became a fearless evangelist. In her memoirs, Sister Lucia describes Jacinta—who, remember, was not quite ten years old when she died—as "always serious and reserved, but friendly."[153]

This was after the apparitions. Before them, she was "the personification of enthusiasm and caprice."[154] But afterward, Jacinta was never afraid to admonish anyone, no matter their age, if they did or said anything inappropriate. She would tell

[151] Ibid., 50.
[152] Ibid.
[153] Ibid., 186.
[154] Ibid.

them, "Don't do that, for you are offending the Lord our God, and He is already so much offended."[155]

Her fearlessness should make us examine ourselves and how we might react in those kinds of situations. At the same time, if Jacinta spotted a log in her own eye or unwittingly offended someone, she would go the extra mile to make up for it, while simultaneously putting the Fatima requests into practice. A perfect example is the time when she was ill and refused the milk her mother wanted her to drink. Lucia revealed that Jacinta "was not fond of milk."

At that time, Lucia, who was visiting her ill younger cousin, asked how she could disobey her mother and not offer up drinking that milk as a sacrifice to the Lord. Jacinta immediately expressed she was sorry, cried, and admitted that she forgot. She called her mother right away to tell her she was sorry and to ask forgiveness, and she agreed to take whatever her mother wanted to her to have.

Back came her mother with the milk, and "Jacinta drank it down without the slightest sign of repugnance." Afterward, she told Lucia, "If you only knew how hard it was to drink that."[156] But it did not stop there. After that, she continued to drink the milk her mother brought her. It never got easier, but she did it for the same reason — to offer it up in reparation.

In the culture that has developed a century after the apparitions, it's quite difficult to fathom that one so young, a child, would willingly suffer. But more than once, Jacinta did so, and she gave the reason why.

[155] Ibid., 187.
[156] Memoirs, 59.

When Lucia asked her if she was suffering very much, Jacinta told her that she was, explaining, "But I offer everything for sinners and in reparation to the Immaculate Heart of Mary." She would continue to do so, willingly and ardently. She told Lucia that Jesus and Mary "greatly love those who suffer for the conversion of sinners."[157]

Jacinta would also prompt her cousin and her brother Francisco to pray for sinners with her. "We must pray very much, to save souls from hell!" she would repeat. "So many go there! So many!"[158]

Of course, when we pray the Rosary, we add a prayer after every decade, which Our Lady of Fatima taught us: "O my Jesus, forgive us our sins, save us from the fires of hell; lead all souls to heaven, especially those who have most need of Your mercy." Much later, in a letter written in 1941, Lucia would explain who she believed were meant by those "most in need." She affirmed, "I believe that Our Lady referred to the souls who are in the most danger of being condemned."[159]

To help as many as she could to avoid the terrible fate of hell, Jacinta spent great amounts of time praying for those in danger of damnation. She wondered why Our Lady hadn't shown the same vision of hell she had shown them to sinners and to all people, especially the droves who came to the Cova for the apparitions.

"If they saw it, they would not sin, so as to avoid going there," she would say. "You must tell Our Lady to show hell to all the people. You'll see how they will be converted."[160]

---

[157] Ibid., 61.
[158] Ibid., 125.
[159] Martins, *Documents on Fatima*, 397.
[160] *Memoirs*, 125.

Lucia also wrote telling her bishop that there are people, "even devout ones, who sometimes are afraid to speak about hell to the children lest they frighten them, but God did not hesitate to show it to three children."[161] Yet how many adults have not heard about it?

Lucia reflected on two important points here about Jacinta and her penances. She believed that Jacinta was able to do these things because God bestowed on her a special grace, through the Immaculate Heart of Mary; and also because she "had looked upon hell and had seen the ruin of souls who fall therein."[162]

Jacinta willingly suffered to save souls. Before she went to the hospital in Lisbon where she would die, she would hug the crucifix, kiss it, and say, "O my Jesus! I love You, and I want to suffer very much for love of You." At other times, "O Jesus! Now You can convert many sinners because this is really a big sacrifice!"

In light of the Fatima message, Jacinta's actions should make us ask if we do [163]enough for the conversion of sinners, as Our Lady requested.

We should also remind ourselves now and then that, when we end each decade of the Rosary, which we should pray daily, as Our Lady requested, we are following the same path and praying for souls in peril, as Jacinta, Lucia, and Francisco faithfully did.

Our Blessed Mother Visits Jacinta

Often forgotten or never realized is the fact that, outside the Fatima apparitions themselves, Our Lady visited Jacinta a number of times. Lucia revealed details of some of these visits.

---

[161] Martins, *Documents on Fatima*, 404.

[162] *Memoirs*, 125.

[163] Ibid., 62.

One included Francisco when he and his sister Jacinta were ill, both having caught the Spanish flu. Even as a nine-year-old, Jacinta was willing to suffer greatly.

One day, she asked to have Lucia visit her at Francisco's bedside, where she had been keeping him company. When Lucia got there, Jacinta told her that Our Lady had come to see them.

"She told us she would come to take Francisco to heaven very soon, and she asked me if I still wanted to convert more sinners. I said I did," Jacinta reported to her cousin. Then she continued, "She told me I would be going to a hospital where I would suffer a great deal and that I am to suffer for the conversion of sinners, in reparation for the sins committed against the Immaculate Heart of Mary, and for love of Jesus."[164]

When Jacinta asked the Blessed Mother if Lucia would accompany her to the hospital, Our Lady told her that she would not. Jacinta told Lucia, "That is what I find hardest. She said my mother would take me, and then I would have to stay there all alone!" She stopped, mulling this over, and then said, "If only you could be with me! The hardest part is to go without you.... I'll be there suffering all alone! But never mind. I'll suffer for love of Our Lord, to make reparation to the Immaculate Heart of Mary, for the conversion of sinners, and for the Holy Father."[165]

As Jacinta's illness grew worse, our Blessed Mother again visited this young child in the hospital. It was to tell her, who was so much advanced spiritually beyond her years, that there were more sacrifices and crosses coming.

Jacinta shared the details of the visit with her older cousin: "She told me that I am going to Lisbon to another hospital; that

---

[164] Memoirs, 59–60.
[165] Ibid., 60.

I will not see you again, nor my parents either, and after suffering a great deal, I shall die alone. But she said I must not be afraid, since she herself is coming to take me to heaven." Crying, she continued, "I will never see you again. You won't be coming to visit me there. Oh, please, pray hard for me, because I am going to die alone!"[166]

Suffering as she was, that special grace from God and Our Lady carried Jacinta along. "Let me think about it," she would tell her cousin, "for the more I think, the more I suffer, and I want to suffer for love of Our Lord and for sinners. Anyway, I don't mind! Our Lady will come to me there and take me to heaven."[167]

When she was very thirsty, she did not even want to take water because she was offering this extra suffering to Jesus for the conversion of sinners.

Jacinta would even comfort her parents. She told her mother not to worry because she was going to heaven and would there be praying for her and the family.

Jacinta's Mystical Insights

Although just a child, Jacinta was a mystic, given a number of insights from heaven.

Lucia recalls the day when Jacinta had her vision of a suffering pontiff. Jacinta said she saw the Holy Father "in a very big house, kneeling by a table, with his head buried in his hands, and he was weeping. Outside the house, there were many people. Some of them were throwing stones, others were cursing him and using bad language. Poor Holy Father, we must pray a lot for him."[168]

---

[166] Ibid., 62.
[167] Ibid.
[168] Martins, *Documents of Fatima*, 407.

Another time, at prayer with the other two children outdoors, Jacinta rose and said, "Can't you see all those highways and roads and fields full of people, who are crying with hunger and have nothing to eat? And the Holy Father in a church praying before the Immaculate Heart of Mary? And so many people praying with him?"[169]

She would also be very upset by the visions she later received of the second terrible war that would erupt if people did not do as Our Lady said. When her cousin asked what she was so sad and upset about, she answered, "About the war which is coming, and all the people who are going to die and go to hell! How dreadful! If they would only stop offending God, then there wouldn't be any war, and they wouldn't go to hell!"[170]

Jacinta became like some child prophet, warning us against sin. She provided proverb-like lessons and admonitions about the need to stay on the narrow road and what people might suffer should they wander onto the wide road that Our Lord spoke of. A significant incident happened while Jacinta was in a Lisbon institute for exceptionally ill children, the orphanage on the Rua da Estrela, run by a kindly nun named Mother Godinho. There, Jacinta received visits from Our Lady.

It was no coincidence that Jacinta spent time in this orphanage on the street named Estrela before being moved to a hospital. She had poetic names for many things in nature that she loved. Jacinta called the stars "the angels' lanterns," and to her, the sun's soft light on hills at evening was "our Lady's lamp."[171]

---

[169] *Memoirs*, 129.
[170] Ibid., 130.
[171] De Marchi, *True Story*, 16.

The place where she stayed was right by the Basilica da Estrela, and from one window, she could see the city's Estrela gardens, where she could watch the birds.

What might all this mean? And how does it fit? And what might this tell us? Heaven doesn't do things by coincidence. "Estrela" is the Portuguese word for "star." It was a heavenly sign that the angels were sent to watch over her.

At the orphanage, Jacinta received mystical insights, which Father di Marchi lists in his book. Among them are these:

- The sins that cause most souls to go to hell are the sins of the flesh.
- Fashions will much offend our Lord. People who serve God should not follow the fashions. The Church has no fashions. Our Lord is always the same.
- The sins of the world are very great.
- If men knew what eternity is, they would do everything to change their lives.
- People are lost because they do not think of the death of our Lord, and do not do penance.
- Many marriages are not of God, and do not please our Lord.
- Wars are the punishments for sin.
- Our Lady cannot at present avert the justice of her Son from the world.
- Penance is necessary. If people amend their lives, our Lord will even yet save the world, but if not, punishment will come.
- You must pray much for sinners and for priests and religious. Priests should concern themselves only with the things of the Church.
- Priests must be very, very pure.

- Disobedience of priests and religious to their superiors displeases our Lord very much.
- Heaven forgive those who persecute the Church of Christ.
- If the government would leave the Church in peace and give liberty to our holy religion, it would have God's blessing.

On Christian virtues:

- Mother, fly from riches and luxury.
- Love poverty and silence.
- Have charity, even for bad people.
- Do not speak evil of people, and fly from evil speakers.
- Mortification and sacrifice please our Lord very much.
- Confession is a sacrament of mercy, and we must confess with joy and trust. There can be no salvation without confession.
- The Mother of God wants more virgin souls bound by a vow of chastity.
- To be pure in body means to be chaste, and to be pure in mind means not to commit sins; not to look at what one should not see, not to steal or lie, and always to speak the truth, even if it is hard.
- Doctors do not know how to cure people properly because they have not the love of God.[172]

When Mother Godhina asked Jacinta who taught her all this, she answered, "Our Lady, but some of them I thought out myself. I love to think."[173]

Jacinta revealed that Our Lady had appeared to her and emphasized the pervasiveness of "sins of luxury and carnality that

---

[172] De Marchi, *True Story*, 158–159.
[173] Ibid., 160.

cost the loss of so many souls."[174] The Queen of Heaven was asking for penance in reparation for those sins.

If such vices were prevalent then, have they not multiplied many times over a century later? We could spend a chapter on just a few of them, showing how much they spread and increased in the later twentieth century and continue to increase today.

Jacinta Is Incorrupt

Jacinta is incorrupt. She's one of the few saints whose bodies (or some body parts) are incorrupt. It surely can be taken as a heavenly gift in light of her holiness. And there were other miraculous signs surrounding her death.

Jacinta died on Friday, February 20, 1920, a few weeks short of her tenth birthday. The doctor who had tended to her thought it best not to bury her immediately in light of the apparitions that had occurred. He suggested that she be brought to the Church of the Holy Angels until she could be moved to a vault somewhere.

As soon as people heard where she was, spontaneous pilgrimages sprang up. People wanted to pray by her and touch statues and rosaries to her.

In the meantime, a suitable vault was offered by a baron and his family at Vila Nova de Ourém, but that meant days of delay until all the arrangements could be made. And the funeral was not to be held until Tuesday.

All this time, Jacinta's casket stayed open as visitors kept flowing in to see her and pray by her. She was dressed in a white First Communion dress and blue sash, the colors of the Blessed Mother, as Jacinta herself requested. Only when the priest attending her became worried about the city's sanitation

[174] Ibid., 161.

ordinances did he have the casket locked up in a room in the church. Because of the devastating flu epidemic, sanitation laws were very strict.

Yet the pilgrims' petition to see her prevailed, and the funeral director brought them in smaller groups into that room. The people were so devoted, they even kissed Jacinta. Many would attest that, during this time, Jacinta's cheeks remained "with live pinkness," and her whole body exhaled a "beautiful aroma of flowers."[175]

The devout call it "the odor of sanctity," and there were more who claimed, "It is the perfume of the Virgin."

"It was that same delightful fragrance that streamed three years previously from the branches stripped by the children from the tree in Valinhos, where the Virgin appeared, following their imprisonment."[176] Remember, there was no embalming at that time, and Jacinta had been there for several days. Her sickness should have produced a rather less-than-pleasant odor. Instead, the saintly child, like Padre Pio, emitted the odor of sanctity. Then, when Jacinta was entombed in the vault in Vila Nova de Ourém, her body was sprinkled with quicklime because, at the time, the law stated that the body of anyone who died of the Spanish flu epidemic had to be treated that way.

Yet when her tomb was opened years later, on September 13, 1935, the people were astonished to see that her features were incorrupt. Preserved this way, she was reburied next to her brother Francisco in the Fatima cemetery.

Heaven was surely rewarding Jacinta and confirming the unsullied sanctity of this young child.

---

[175] Ibid., 164.
[176] Cappa, *Fatima: Cove of Wonders*, 243.

The Fruits of Fatima

Francisco

Francisco got a lesson very quickly on the importance of the Rosary, and it's a lesson that speaks to us today. During the first apparition on May 13, 1917, Francisco was the only one of the three children who could not see Our Lady. He knew his cousin Lucia and his sister Jacinta were seeing something extraordinary. But why didn't he see her? How could he see what they saw?

"Our Lady then told Lucia to tell Francisco to say the Rosary, and he would see the beautiful Lady from heaven," recounted Fatima expert Father Robert J. Fox in *The Spirituality of Francisco Marto*.[177]

Francisco listened. He held his rosary, and after he had said five or six Hail Marys, he could see "the beautiful heavenly Lady bathed in brilliant light, brighter than the sun," writes Father Fox. "Was not Our Lady in this incident again leading Francisco to become more of the contemplative? He must think, inquire, pray."[178]

Francisco could now see but could not hear Our Lady as Lucia and Jacinta could. When Lucia asked if he would go to heaven, too, Our Lady answered, "Yes, but first he must say many Rosaries." Lucia repeated her answer to Francisco. Excitedly, he said, "Oh, Our Lady, I will say all the Rosaries you wish!"[179]

Put simply, Francisco's eyes were opened as soon as he began listening to the request of Our Lady that day. He was able to "see" the importance of what she asked when he started praying the Rosary.

---

[177] Fr. Robert J. Fox, "The Spirituality of Francisco Marto," Soul, (July–August 1996), EWTN, www.ewtn.com/library/MARY/FMARTO.htm.

[178] Ibid.

[179] Ibid.

Of course, Francisco didn't stop after this initial directive. He grew in the practice. Father Fox asked Francisco's brother, Joao Marto, if, as children, he thought Francisco was holier than he. Joao told him, "No. Not until I noticed he was always saying the Rosary. Then I would go and hide from him so that I didn't have to see him always praying that Rosary."[180]

Let's not follow the example of Francisco's brother and "hide" when we hear about praying the Rosary.

Like saints of old, Francisco spent hours in prayer. It was not necessary for him and his sister Jacinta to learn to read, since, during the second apparition, on June 13, the Blessed Mother told Lucia that she would take them to heaven soon.

Not having to learn to read didn't bother Francisco at all. It only opened more time for him to pray. Although he was only nine when the apparitions began, he, like his sister, became a mystic. In her memoirs, Lucia reveals how her young cousin, the saint-to-be, loved solitude and prayer. He spoke little and often kept to himself the sacrifices he made.

According to Lucia, he liked to slip away to pray and meditate, to "think and console Our Lord, who is so sad" because of so many sins. On the way to school, he would tell Lucia to go on ahead of him, but he would stay in church with the Hidden Jesus. "It's not worth my while learning to read," he said, "as I'll be going to heaven very soon."[181]

He loved to spend time in prayer in the church. There he would first console the Hidden Jesus and then pray for the conversion of sinners.

---

[180] Ibid.
[181] *Memoirs*, 156.

The Fruits of Fatima

For someone so young, Francisco became quite a contemplative. Lucia once asked him what he liked best — to console Our Lord or to convert sinners to prevent them from going to hell. Francisco did not have to hesitate to answer that question.

"I prefer to console Our Lord," he said. "Don't you remember last month how Our Lady became so sad when she asked us not to offend Our Lord, who was already so offended? I want to console Our Lord and then to convert sinners so that they won't offend Him anymore."[182] Francisco's preference expressed here harmoniously complements his sister's personal emphasis on prayer for the salvation of sinners.

Francisco might have lived in a small hamlet, but his actions and words have traveled afar and should reverberate around the world because they're all in tune with Fatima, showing us the importance of prayer and the need to turn from sin.

Even during the time of the apparitions, Francisco showed the courage of a saint. That example came just before the fourth apparition on August 13, when he, Jacinta, and Lucia were kidnapped and taken to prison in Ourém, and the three remained firm in the face of death threats.

As it grew late, the children were given a meal and locked in a room overnight. The next day, the administrator ramped up his tactics. The children were separated to be questioned and threatened, as if that would break down the resistance of at least one of them. When no threat or intimidation worked, the children were tossed into a cell with a crew of criminals.

"Don't cry, Jacinta. We can offer this to Jesus for sinners," Francisco told his sister. Then he started to pray the prayer Our

---

[182] Fox, "The Spirituality of Francisco Marto."

Lady taught them, "O my Jesus, this is for love of You, and for the conversion of sinners."[183]

Jacinta chimed in, "And also for the Holy Father, and in reparation for the sins committed against the Immaculate Heart of Mary."

And when Francisco was waiting his turn during the individual interrogations, he was full of joy and peace. He said, "If they kill us as they say, we'll soon be in heaven. How wonderful! Nothing else matters! — God grant that Jacinta won't be afraid. I'm going to say a Hail Mary for her!"[184]

We can't chalk this reaction up to naïveté, not in the face of death threats and the rough treatment already endured. It was enough to scare the wits out of an adult. But Francisco's courage shows that grace was given to him in abundance as he grew in prayer and the virtue of fortitude. He didn't remain stagnant in his spiritual life, and neither will anyone else who follows the path pointed out by Our Lady at Fatima.

At the same time, Francisco retained his childlike qualities. He had a fondness for birds, and he was concerned for their welfare. As Lucia observed, he "could not bear to see anyone robbing their nests."[185] He would save some of the bread he had for lunch and put the crumbs on top of rocks so the birds could come and have their fill.

Lucia also described how he would talk with them: "Poor wee things! You are hungry. Come and eat!"[186] And they would flock around him. He was living up to his namesake, St. Francis of Assisi.

[183] *Memoirs,* 52; Haffert, *Russia Will Be Converted,* 45–46.
[184] *Memoirs,* 148.
[185] Ibid., 158.
[186] Ibid., 159.

The Fruits of Fatima

Of course, people and their spiritual welfare were of primary importance to Francisco even though he preferred solitude. One day, a woman from a village a mile and a half away came to see Francisco, who, at the time, was very ill and confined to his room. The poor woman was beside herself with grief. Because of a problem with their son, her husband had forced the young man out of the family home. The son refused to listen to and live by the conditions his father had set for the house. The son had been asking his father to pardon him, but the father kept refusing, since the young man still rejected the conditions set down. The woman wanted help from Francisco to obtain the grace of reconciliation between the father and the son.

"Don't worry. I'm going to heaven very soon, and when I get there, I will ask Our Lady for that grace," Francisco told her.[187] And not long after making this promise, he died.

Lucia remembered perfectly that on the very afternoon of the day Francisco went to heaven, the son made one final attempt to reconcile with his father. He agreed to accept all that his father required, and they immediately reconciled. The home once again became peaceful.

As a side note, that young man's sister eventually married the brother of Francisco and Jacinta. Their daughter later joined the Dorothean Sisters, the community Lucia first entered. Francisco's intercessory prayer clearly had a major ripple effect in the family. If following the teaching and motherly directives of Our Lady at Fatima set the children on such paths, just think of what her advice can do for every one of those who follow the same route.

The saintly example of the brother and sister Fatima seers shows us that anyone, even a child, can become a saint. The sanctity of

---

[187] Ibid., 192.

those young ones became recognized by the Church rather quickly. Even before Francisco and Jacinta were canonized as the youngest nonmartyrs in the Church's two-thousand-year history on the one hundredth anniversary of the first Fatima apparition, they became two of the youngest Blesseds ever named, when, on May 13, 2000, Pope John Paul II traveled to Fatima to beatify them.

"Devoting themselves with total generosity to such a good Teacher," John Paul II said, "Jacinta and Francisco soon reached the heights of perfection." The little shepherds became saints quickly by going "to Jesus through Mary," which saints such as Louis de Montfort and John Paul II himself have taught and lived. And this proves that even children can do it.

How many people in the last hundred years have taken to heart the messages and requests of Our Lady at Fatima and tried to follow them — even after hearing about them from more than one Holy Father? But the young seers, during their short lives, were already doing just that and, in a way, anticipating what Pope Pius XII would teach years later. "He [Jesus] wills to be helped by the members of His Body in carrying out the work of redemption," Pius XII writes in *Mystici Corporis*. He goes on to say:

> This is a deep mystery and an inexhaustible subject of meditation that the salvation of many depends on the prayers and voluntary penances which the members of the Mystical Body of Jesus Christ offer for this intention and on the cooperation of pastors of souls and of the faithful, especially of fathers and mothers of families, a cooperation which they must offer to our Divine Savior as though they were His associates.[188]

[188] Pius XII, Encyclical Letter *Mystici Corporis* (June 29, 1943), no. 44.

As for one of her mortifications and sacrifices to help sinners, Jacinta would willingly give up food. And when she was ill, she still went to Mass on weekdays, although Lucia would tell her not to go but to rest.

"That doesn't matter! I'm going for sinners who don't go on a Sunday," she said.[189]

During his homily at Fatima on May 13, 2000, Pope Benedict XVI commended this saintly child with these words: "Blessed Jacinta, in particular, proved tireless in sharing with the needy and in making sacrifices for the conversion of sinners. Only with this fraternal and generous love will we succeed in building the civilization of love and peace."

Although the three children weren't meditating on what St. Paul said — "Now I rejoice in my sufferings for your sake, and in my flesh I am filling up what is lacking in the afflictions of Christ on behalf of his body, which is the church" (Col. 1:24) — they surely were putting it into practice. Or, as Father di Marchi explained, "The vision of hell that they had seen in July was not erased from their minds. They prayed incessantly. They sought new sacrifice. Praying the Rosary, they never forgot to include the prayer after each decade Our Lady taught them to say": *O my Jesus, forgive us our sins, save us from the fires of hell; lead all souls to heaven, especially those who have most need of Your mercy.*[190]

It's such a simple prayer to learn and to say after each decade of the Rosary, yet do we? We must pray for Our Lord's mercy for ourselves and for others, especially those who are in dire need of it. It is a spiritual work of mercy on our part.

---

[189] *Memoirs*, 126.
[190] De Marchi, *True Story*, 71.

Lucia

There was something special about Lucia from her earliest years. She was born on March 28, 1907.

As a little child, Lucia was spiritually precocious. She got special permission to receive her First Holy Communion at age six — a year earlier than usual for children at that time — since she knew her catechism and explained the mystery of the Eucharist so well.

In her second memoir, Lucia explains that the day before receiving her First Holy Communion, right after her first Confession, she knelt in front of a statue of Our Lady of the Rosary to pray. When she asked Our Lady to keep her "poor heart for God alone," she writes, "I saw the Mother smile! I heard her 'Yes!' And I heard the sound of her voice: 'My daughter, the grace that is given to you today will remain forever alive in your heart, producing fruits of eternal life.'"[191]

Though her cousins died at early age, Lucia would live into her nineties. It was her job to bring the messages of Our Lady of Fatima to the world. Our Lady prepared her for this mission during the June 13, 1917, apparition when she told Lucia, "I want you to come on the thirteenth of next month, to pray the Rosary every day, and to learn to read and write. Later, I will tell you what I want."

The request was unusual, since girls in her situation didn't learn to read. But as Father Andrew Apostoli explains in his book *Fatima for Today*, since it was Lucia's mission to spread the Fatima message to the world, it was crucial that she be able to read and write. In later years, she even used the word processor. Among Sister Lucia's writings are voluminous letters and her

---

[191] *Memoirs*, 71; Carmel of Coimbra, *A Pathway*, 38.

books, which include *"Calls" from the Message of Fatima* and her two-volume memoirs, *Fatima in Lucia's Own Words*, written under obedience. Lucia would begin her writing when she entered the convent.

After Our Lady told Lucia that she was to learn to read and write, she revealed the young girl's mission, saying that, while Jacinta and Francisco would soon be brought to heaven, Lucia would remain in the world.

"Jesus wishes you to make me known and loved on earth," Our Lady said. "He wishes also for you to establish devotion in the world to my Immaculate Heart."

And when Lucia again asked, "Must I remain in the world alone?" Our Lady consoled her: "Not alone, my child, and you must not be sad. I will be with you always, and my Immaculate Heart will be your comfort and the way which will lead you to God."

How often we forget that this last sentence our Blessed Mother said to Lucia also applies to every one of us as we follow our Mother. Saints before this time knew it. We should not let this truth of Fatima easily slip past us. We, too, should desire to be comforted by the Immaculate Heart and led to God by Mary.

Because of their closeness to Our Lady, Lucia and her cousins were often sought out by members of the surrounding communities. On September 8, 1917, a young man visited Lucia's home to speak with her. Lucia describes her first reaction:

> He was of such tall stature that I trembled with fear. When I saw that he had to bend down in order to come through the doorway in search of me, I thought I must be in the presence of a German. At that time we were at war, and grown-ups would try to frighten children by saying, "Here comes a German to kill you."

I thought, therefore, that my last hour had come. My fright did not pass unnoticed by the young man, who sought to calm me; he made me sit on his knee and questioned me with great kindness.[192]

The man then asked Lucia's mother if the child could show him the apparition site and pray there with him. She agreed. All along the way Lucia was fearful, but she writes, "Then I began to feel tranquil again at the thought that if he killed me, I would go to see Our Lord and Our Lady."[193]

At the site, the man knelt and asked Lucia to pray the Rosary with him to receive a special grace from Our Lady — that a young lady he knew would consent to become his wife. Lucia recalled thinking at the moment, "If she has as much fear of him as I, she will never say yes!"[194]

After the Rosary, the young man walked Lucia home and, saying goodbye, asked her to pray for his request.

A month later, on October 13, at the site of the last apparition, Lucia got two great surprises. She describes the first: "I suddenly found myself, after the apparitions, in the arms of this same person, sailing along over the heads of the people. It actually served to satisfy the curiosity of everybody who wanted to see me!"[195]

Maneuvering through the crowd, the young man stumbled and fell. But Lucia was caught in the crush of people pressing around her. "Right away, others took hold of me, and this gentleman disappeared," she said.[196]

---

[192] *Memoirs*, 96.
[193] Ibid., 97.
[194] Ibid.
[195] Ibid.
[196] Ibid.

Then came the second surprise when "he appeared again, this time accompanied by the aforesaid girl, who was now his wife!" Lucia says. "He came to thank the Blessed Virgin for the grace received and to ask her copious blessings on their future. This young man is today Dr. Carlos Mendes of Torres Novas."[197]

Incidents such as this were not unusual when it came to the children. Such occurrences were surely providential, like little indicators of the hands of heaven that came upon the children and the Fatima area.

Endless individuals and groups constantly sought Lucia until she was finally sent anonymously to a convent school. At the school, she thrived and quickly realized that the religious life was for her. She first became a Dorothean Sister, but on March 25, 1948, she entered the Carmel in Coimbra, not far from Fatima. The solemnity of the Annunciation would usually be celebrated on that date, but that year it was Holy Thursday. This was quite fitting, as Lucia was born on a Holy Thursday. Sister Lucia would live here as a Carmelite nun until her death on February 13, 2005.

On her entrance into Carmel at Coimbra, Lucia was given the name Sister Mary of the Immaculate Heart. Although Bishop Serafim de Sousa Ferreira e Silva, bishop of Leiria-Fatima, referred to her as Sister Lucia, he noted also that her full religious name is Sister Maria Lucia of Jesus and of the Immaculate Heart.

At Carmel, the cell Lucia received was dedicated to the Immaculate Heart of Mary, as noted on a sign above the door. It carried the additional sentence: "My Immaculate Heart will be your refuge."[198] The Immaculate Heart had been precisely that and would remain so for Lucia as she lived in the Carmelite convent

[197] Ibid.
[198] Carmel of Coimbra, A Pathway, 311.

for the next fifty-seven years. In her later years, Sister Lucia had in her cell a statue of Our Lady of Fatima that she cherished dearly. It was a gift to her from Pope John Paul II, given in 2003.

While we know from all that Lucia told us that Jacinta became more and more serious after the apparitions in her suffering and sacrifices for the conversion of sinners, on the other hand, we learn from sources such as *A Pathway under the Gaze of Mary*, written by the Carmelite nuns who lived with Sister Lucia, that she would joke even when she was in her nineties and very ill.

Dr. Branca Paul, the physician who attended Lucia for the last fifteen years of her life, also said, "It was amazing that she was so normal, simple, and humble. Full of joy and laughter, always joking and smiling a lot.... Sister Lucia was great to be around. Her infectious joy made everyone happier."

She gives an example from when Lucia was ninety-seven. "She accepted her age very well. Once, when I came to give her a checkup, I asked her if there was anything she wanted. 'Oh, Dr. Branca, make me 30 again!' She then burst out laughing. That was Sr. Lucia. She never complained. She accepted everything."[199]

Lucia's cheerful spirit, despite the suffering she underwent for the sake of sinners, was an example of Jesus' directive: "But when you fast, anoint your head and wash your face, so that you may not appear to others to be fasting, except to your Father who is hidden. And your Father who sees what is hidden will repay you" (Matt. 6:17–18).

Dr. Paul wasn't the only one who saw those qualities in Lucia. Father John de Marchi, who knew Sister Lucia well, described her as "an absolutely normal personality and ... as real as a plate of cookies ... and if I were obliged to point out her outstanding

[199] Ibid.

natural characteristic, I would say it was her gaiety. No one has been able to detect in her the least sign of morbid temperament or exclusive self-concern."[200] Lucia had a lighthearted way and knew how to be humorous, too. She wasn't a long-faced nun.

Lucia might not have bilocated, as it appears her younger cousin Jacinta did, but, like her cousin, she was extraordinarily heroic in helping people. In fact, when she was a Dorothean Sister and known as Sister Dores, she saved two children from drowning. Lucia's doctor had ordered her to spend a month at the seaside, resting and taking sea baths to regain her health. Since other Sisters also needed the sea air for their ills, the mother provincial rented a house for them.

One morning on the beach, some women were collecting seaweed while their two children played in the sand. Normally calm, the sea was quite strong that day. Lucia had climbed some rocks and was harvesting shellfish when she heard screams and cries of distress from the women. A strong wave had swept up the children and was pulling them from the shore.

Lucia immediately jumped into the water.

"I managed to grab one of the children and bring her out," Lucia later wrote, describing the harrowing incident.

At first, I didn't see the other, but soon discovered her leaning on a rock where, fortunately, she was trapped, wedged between rocks. I pulled her out with the help of Our Lady, to whom I called, and managed to save those two lives. After a few agonizing moments during which the children vomited up the sea water they had swallowed, the poor women did not know how to thank me.

[200] De Marchi, *True Story*, 4.

'You have to thank the Virgin that was here and not me,' I told them, to instill in them devotion to Our Lady. In fact, I believed that it was she who helped me because although swimming was easy for me, the affliction was enough to stop me.[201]

Lucia's experience is a beautiful lesson on the need to rely on our Blessed Mother's help and to trust that she will be with us, just as she told Lucia she would be with her. We have to trust in her and call on her. Why would she not be with us? She came to Fatima for us and showed us her motherly love, the same kind of concern she showed for the young married couple at the wedding at Cana.

Because of Our Lady's instructions during the July 13 apparition that Lucia should learn to read, Lucia came to realize that fulfilling her mission would include being a writer. Although she was not keen on writing at first, as we'll see, when she followed our Blessed Mother's wishes and directives, she succeeded tremendously.

Lucia began her writing by putting on paper all her memories, insights, and teachings on Fatima. Her major work began with the first of four memoirs or reminiscences, when she was ordered by Bishop José Alves Correira da Silva of Leiria to record what she remembered about Jacinta.

At the start, while in the Dorothean convent, Lucia had received photos of her cousin taken when Jacinta's remains were moved from Via Nova de Oureém to Fatima and her casket opened. In a 1935 letter, written in thanks for the photos, she said:

---

[201] Carmel of Coimbra, A *Pathway*, 218.

I was half in the clouds, such was my joy at seeing again my closest childhood friend.

I have hopes that Our Lord, for the glory of the Most Holy Virgin, will grant her the crown of sanctity. She was a child only in years. As for the rest, she knew how to practice virtue and to show God and the Most Holy Virgin her love, through the practice of sacrifice. It is to her companionship that I owe, in part, the conservation of my innocence.[202]

When the bishop read this remembrance, he requested that Lucia write down more details. Lucia wrote back that she would take up the work "in spite of the repugnance I feel," but "I obey, nevertheless, the will of Your Excellency, which, for me, is the expression of the will of our good God. I begin this task, then, asking the most holy Hearts of Jesus and Mary to deign to bless it and to make use of this act of obedience to obtain the conversion of poor sinners, for whom Jacinta so generously sacrificed herself."[203]

Thinking of her limitations, she added, "I know that Your Excellency does not expect that I write skillfully because you know my incapacity and insufficiency."

Lucia did not realize her natural gift for bringing the truth to life and for painting vivid pictures in all sincerity and honesty. With the eye of an artist, she described her humble home in orderly and precise detail, taking readers through it with "word photos."

Her spelling and punctuation were imperfect at times, but, as Bishop Serafim de Sousa Ferreira e Silva of Leiria-Fatima wrote

---

[202] Martins, *Documents on Fatima,* 301.
[203] *Memoirs*, 34.

in his preliminary note to her book *"Calls" from the Message of Fatima*, "Our Lady asked her to 'learn to read'; she did not ask her to go to the university!"[204]

Less than two weeks after Lucia began the initial memoir, on Christmas Day 1935, she finished it. At the time, it was titled simply *Jacinta*. Lucia expanded the memoir shortly afterward when a priest working with the bishop suggested he ask Lucia to delve further into the history and details of the apparitions. The bishop made the request.

Lucia started this work on November 7, 1937, completing the second memoir by November 21. Included are accounts of the apparitions of the angel and the revelation of the Immaculate Heart of Mary in the June apparition, plus several other details.

Her writings are "exceptionally transparent and unpretentious," Father Louis Kondor noted in the introduction to the collected memoirs, *Fatima in Lucia's Own Words*.

With Fatima's silver jubilee in 1942 on the horizon, the bishop wanted Lucia to write further. This expanded version of what was then known as *Jacinta* would be the third memoir and would be completed in time for the jubilee. Lucia realized that this was the time to reveal the First and Second Secrets of Fatima.

She wrote the bishop:

> The moment has arrived to reply to two questions which have often been sent to me, but which I have put off answering until now.
>
> In my opinion, it would be pleasing to God and to the Immaculate Heart of Mary that, in the book *Jacinta*, one chapter would be devoted to the subject of hell and

---

[204] *"Calls,"* 4.

another to the Immaculate Heart of Mary. Your Excellency will indeed find this opinion rather strange and perhaps inopportune, but it is not my own idea. God Himself will make clear to you that this is a matter that pertains to his glory and to the good of souls.[205]

These updates were written in the summer of 1941. After Lucia completed the text, the bishop and a priest working closely on Fatima with him visited her on the feast of the Holy Rosary, wanting to know more. She wrote the next texts in two parts, turning in the first part on November 5 and the second on December 8, the solemnity of the Immaculate Conception.

Over the years, after finally completing her memoirs (she was asked years later to write a fifth about her father and a sixth about her mother), Lucia continued her efforts as a writer. She penned not only a book — *"Calls" from the Message of Fatima* — but thousands of letters, most from the decades she lived in the Carmel in Coimbra.

In his introduction to *Fatima in Lucia's Own Words*, Father Kondor explains that Lucia's deficiencies in things such as spelling did not hamper her "clear and distinct construction of sentences; sometimes, indeed, she writes in an elegant and elevated style."

Father Kondor summarizes Lucia's literary qualities in this way:

Accuracy and clarity of thought; delicate and deep feeling; lively imagination and a truly artistic sense of humor, giving charm to the narrative; a sensitive irony that never hurts; an extraordinary memory as far as details and circumstances are concerned. Lucia's dialogues pour

---

[205] *Memoirs*, 122.

forth as though the people concerned were present in person. In her imagination, she sees the scenery as if it were before her eyes. She describes Jacinta and Francisco, her confessors, and others, with words which disclose an unusual psychological insight. She is fully conscious of her deviations and always returns with much skill to her starting point.[206]

Take one simple sentence in which Lucia draws on Genesis and the Gospel in relation to her efforts. As she turned in the fourth memoir, she wrote to the bishop, saying, "Yielding blindly to the Heavenly Father and to the protection of the Immaculate Heart of Mary, I am going to put into your hands the fruits of my one tree, the tree of obedience."[207]

Father Kondor wasn't the only one to admire and praise Sister Lucia's writings and the way she wove her insights on Fatima and the Sacred Scriptures into a tapestry of spirituality.

"Lucia has sketched out a kind of message of Fatima according to the Gospel, or a Gospel according to Fatima," noted Carmelite Father Jesus Castellano Cervera about *"Calls" from the Message of Fatima.*[208] At the time, he was a consultor of the Congregation for the Doctrine of the Faith.

Father Cervera pointed out how Lucia wrote with "great simplicity and openness" and at the same time with amazing depth and understanding. Over half of the book's text "consists in explicit or implicit references to sacred Scripture. Lucia is very much at home in the books of the Bible."[209]

---

[206] *Memoirs*, 11.
[207] Ibid., 136.
[208] *"Calls,"* 8.
[209] Ibid.

Father Cervera also noted that her book is "easy to read on account of the coherence and simplicity of the themes discussed and their applications."[210] Not only that, but at times her writing "takes on a poetic tone, especially when she praises the beauty of God in creation."[211] He calls the book a catechism of Fatima.

Bishop Ferreira e Silva observed that this book, written entirely by Sister Lucia, is "in effect, a long letter ... in catechetical style" to help those desiring "greater fidelity in living up to what was asked for from heaven in the Cova da Iria."[212]

Lucia was gifted from heaven with her talent for writing. From topic to topic, she offers lessons and insights about Fatima that deepen our love for Our Lady and her Son, Jesus. No doubt Our Lady guided Sister Lucia in remarkable ways as she used her writing ability to further the Fatima message in every way possible.

Lucia's Letters

With all the questions Lucia was constantly asked about Fatima and the messages, she wrote scores of letters in response during her time in the convent—thousands of correspondences. A tiny sample gives us insight into her deep spirituality, especially in relation to Fatima and the message she so urgently and earnestly wanted to spread, and to live herself.

There are a few early letters to a superior, Father Gonzalves, that show her concern for our need to heed Our Lady of Fatima's messages. On April 24, 1940, she wrote:

[210] Ibid., 10.
[211] Ibid., 11.
[212] Ibid, 3.

Sometimes He is displeased not only by our serious sins but also by our laxity and negligence in attending to His requests.

In this regard I am very guilty because of my shyness and reserve. Talk to Him for a while, and you will see what He said. How many just complaints He has to which we cannot answer anything except to ask for forgiveness and this intimate conversation! He's right, there are many crimes, but above all there is much more negligence now on the part of souls, whom He expected to do His work with fervor.

Your least servant,
Maria Lucia de Jesus, r.s.D.

Again, she showed her humility despite her unquestionable depth of spirituality and fervor. She wrote, "I'm in that group of lukewarm people, after the efforts that He has made to incorporate me in the group of those more fervent. It is very easy for me to make a promise, but it is even easier for me to break it.... Dust sticks to actions like it does to [clothes], without one seeing how it got there. But He still is patient, and that's what helps me."[213]

As World War II was raging in Europe, Lucia wrote on July 15, 1940:

Our good Lord could, through some prodigy, show clearly that it is He who asks it, but He takes this opportunity to punish the world with His justice for so many crimes, and to prepare it for a more complete turn toward Him. The proof that He gives us is the special protection of

---

[213] Ibid., 373.

the Immaculate Heart of Mary over Portugal, due to its consecration to Her.

But in our country, there are still many crimes and sins, and since now is the hour of God's justice over the world, we need to keep on praying. For this reason I feel that it would be good to impress on people, as well as a great amount of confidence in the mercy of our good Lord and in the protection of the Immaculate Heart of Mary, the need for prayer accompanied by sacrifice, especially that one needed to avoid sin. This is the request of our good heavenly Mother since 1917, which came with an inexplicable sadness and tenderness from Her Immaculate Heart: *Let them offend our Lord God no more, for He is already much offended.* It's a pity that we have not meditated enough on these words and measured their total reach.

Your least servant,

Maria Lucia de Jesus, r.s.D.[214]

Digressing for a moment from the letters, already in 1937 in her second memoir, Lucia realized:

Of all the words spoken at this Apparition, the ones most deeply engraved upon my heart were those of the request made by our heavenly Mother: do not offend Our Lord and God anymore, because He is already so much offended! How loving a complaint, how tender a request! Who will grant me to make it echo through the whole world, so that all the children of our Mother in heaven may hear the sound of her voice![215]

---

[214] Ibid., 374.

[215] *Memoirs*, 97.

Lucia honed in on this request in her book *"Calls."* The message, she said, reminds us that we must observe the first of all the commandments, the love of God.

If anyone asked her what the Ten Commandments have to do with Fatima, she answered:

> They have a great deal to do with it; they are among the chief aims of the Message. In fact, Our Lady ended the series of apparitions in Fatima with these words: "Do not offend the Lord our God anymore, because He is already so much offended." ... What Our Lady wanted and, therefore the main object of the Message, was to beg us not to offend Our Lord because He was already so deeply offended. There can be no doubt that what offends God most is the breaking of His Law—all Sacred Scripture confirms this.[216]

And as Pope Francis reflected during his visit to Fatima for the hundredth anniversary to canonize Sts. Jacinta and Francisco Marto, "Our Lady foretold and warned us about a way of life that is godless and indeed profanes God in His creatures. Such a life—frequently proposed and imposed—risks leading to hell. Mary came to remind us that God's light dwells within us and protects us."

In a letter she handed to Pope John Paul II during their private meeting on May 13, 1982, Lucia told the saintly Holy Father that Our Lady said that if Russia was consecrated to the Immaculate Heart of Mary,

> Russia will be converted, and there will be peace; if not, she will spread her errors throughout the world, etc.

[216] *"Calls,"* 207.

Since we did not heed this appeal of the Message, we see that it has been fulfilled, Russia has invaded the world with her errors. And if we haven't seen yet the end of this prophecy accomplished, we see that we are going towards it little by little with great strides, if we do not reject the path of sin, hatred, revenge, injustice, violations of the rights of the human person, immorality, and violence, etc.[217]

We cannot say that it is God who punishes us. But rather that it is men who are preparing for themselves the punishment. God warns us and calls us to the right path, while respecting the freedom He gave us; therefore, men are responsible.[218]

During the long homily that John Paul II gave on that day in May 1982 at Fatima, he said this, which fits in with what Lucia was trying to get across: "The greatest obstacle to man's journey toward God is sin, perseverance in sin and, finally, denial of God. The deliberate blotting out of God from the world of human thought; the detachment from Him of the whole of man's earthly activity; the rejection of God by man."

And that was before the turn of the millennium, after which the kind of sin described by the saintly Holy Father only multiplied.

A book by the Carmelite nuns whom Sister Lucia lived with describes the ninety-two-year-old seer going to Fatima to be part of the beatification ceremony for her cousins Jacinta and

---

[217] Congregation for the Doctrine of the Faith, "The Message of Fatima" (June 26, 2000), introduction.
[218] Carmel of Coimbra, A *Pathway*, 189.

Francisco in May 2000. Because John Paul II had decided to reveal the Third Secret of Fatima at that time, he wanted Sister Lucia to testify that she had written the original text on January 3, 1944. She affirmed, "Yes, this is my letter; this text is mine."[219]

The nuns of Sister Lucia's order at Carmel of Coimbra reveal how it always pained her that some people insisted on having the third part of the Secret revealed during all those years when it was still unknown to the public. She would say, "If only they live what is the most important thing, which has already been said.... They only concern themselves with what is left to be said, instead of complying with the request that was prayer and penance!"[220]

That should motivate us to live the requests that Our Lady of the Rosary made plainly for all of us through the seers at Fatima.

More Apparitions to Lucia

Jacinta was not the only one to see our Blessed Mother after the May through October 1917 apparitions. Lucia did also, several times. One of these visits was directly related to the Third Secret of Fatima.

During her first apparition on May 13, Our Blessed Mother promised to return a seventh time. She said, "I want you to return here on the thirteenth of each month for the next six months, and at the very same hour. Later I shall tell you who I am, and what it is that I most desire. And I shall return here yet a seventh time."

There was no consensus about when that seventh time might be. Some thought it might come with another great miracle.

[219] Ibid., 384.
[220] Ibid., 245.

Then came *A Pathway under the Gaze of Mary* in 2013, the biography of Sister Lucia written by the nuns of the Carmel who lived with her for many years. In it, they quote Lucia from a collection of her personal notes called *My Pathway*, which is stored in their archives.

It was June 15, 1921, and Lucia was about to leave Fatima for good to where the bishop wanted to send her. Knowing she would likely never again see the place or her family, she felt unable to go through with leaving. We learn from her notes that she went to the holm oak where the Blessed Mother had appeared, knelt, and prayed in terrible anguish.

Lucia details in *My Pathway*:

> Once again you have come down to Earth; and then I felt your helping hand and maternal touch on my shoulder. I looked up, and I saw you. It was you, Blessed Mother, holding my hand and showing me the path, and your lips unveiled the sweet timbre of your voice, and light and peace was restored to my soul: "Here I am for the seventh time. Go, follow the path which the bishop wants you to take, this is the will of God."[221]

When the bishop of Leiria asked her to write down the Third Secret that Our Lady revealed to the children at Fatima, Sister Lucia hesitated. She wanted to obey the bishop, but she also wanted to obey the orders from heaven about revealing the secret. She made several false starts to write it but could make no progress.

Then, on January 3, 1944, Lucia asked Our Lady to make known the will of God. Then she went as usual to the convent

---

[221] Ibid., 217–218.

chapel, knelt before the tabernacle, and asked the Lord to let her know His will in this situation. She could write anything else easily and without hesitation, but not this.

"I then felt a friendly hand, affectionate and maternal, touch me on the shoulder," Lucia would write in My *Pathway*, later published by the Carmelite nuns in their own book. Lucia then looked up and saw the "beloved Mother from heaven" who said to her, "Do not be afraid. God wanted to prove your obedience, faith, and humility. Be at peace, and write what they order you, but do not give your opinion of its meaning. After writing it, place it in an envelope, close and seal it, and write on the outside that this can only be opened in 1960 by the Cardinal Patriarch of Lisbon or by the Bishop of Leiria."[222]

That is how Lucia received the strength to write the Third Secret.

Lucia also received other visits from Our Lady when she was in the Carmel in Coimbra, but she recorded very few of them. The nuns there learned of some of them, but there were quite possibly other visits she kept to herself. The nuns shared the ones they learned about from Sister Lucia herself, such as the visit of Our Lady on August 22, 1949, to give her a message that she was to relay to the new archbishop of Coimbra, telling him that Our Lady said it was she who chose him.

Another visit took place on December 31, 1979. Sister Lucia was in her cell, suffering and interceding in prayer for the Church, envisioning it like a boat being thrown about on the seas of the world's rebellion against it.

She wrote, "I felt a gentle hand on my left shoulder. I looked, and I saw it was my sweet Mother who had listened to my humble

[222] Ibid., 243.

prayer." Our Lady told her, "God has heard your prayer and sent me to tell you that it is necessary to intensify your prayer and your work for the union of the Church, of the bishops with the Holy Father, and of the priests with the bishops to lead the people of God on the paths of truth, faith, hope and love, united in Christ our Savior."[223]

Lucia said she also received a visit in October 1984 while the community was in their retreat, but she revealed nothing of what took place or what was said during that visit.

Beyond the apparitions of Fatima, these visits of Our Lady to Lucia, and earlier to her cousin Jacinta, strengthened in them what they already knew about Our Lady's requests at Fatima or were in some way related to the seers' continuous spiritual growth. Following the messages of Fatima will strengthen us in our spiritual lives also. Moreover, the Fatima messages are especially vital now with society and the world careening from problem to problem, and morality sliding downhill faster than an Olympic bobsled. At the same time, remember that Our Lady of Fatima's instructions are grounded in the theological virtue of hope. In other words, we can still quickly put the Fatima requests into practice.

[223] Ibid., 352.

8

Why the Daily Rosary?

Why the daily Rosary? That's a good question. We know that the Rosary ranks right after the Mass as the most powerful of prayers. Let's turn to the Fatima seer who gives so many clear reasons why Our Lady insisted on the daily Rosary for all. Servant of God Sister Lucia gives an impeccable explanation in her *"Calls" from the Message of Fatima.*

At Fatima, Our Lady ended her initial message in May with the direction, "Pray the Rosary every day in order to obtain peace for the world and the end of the war."

So crucial and necessary is this call that Lucia devotes a whole section of her book to the Rosary. First, Lucia says, Our Lady of the Rosary gave us this directive to restore peace — in ourselves, with God, in our homes, with neighbors, and among nations.

Next, Sister Lucia mentions how essential it is to pray to receive grace and overcome temptation and how the Rosary is an accessible prayer, not only for the seers, who were children, but for all people.

Sister Lucia, at this time a Carmelite, repeats a question she was asked many times: "Why should Our Lady have told us to say the Rosary every day rather than to attend Mass every day?"

"I cannot be absolutely certain of the answer, as Our Lady did not explain, and it never occurred to me to ask," Lucia answers. But she does go on to share what she thought and came to understand about this call, willingly leaving "all interpretation of the meaning of the Message to Holy Church, because it pertains to the Church to do so; hence I humbly and willingly submit myself to whatever It may wish to say or to correct, amend or declare."[224]

God is a Father who

> adapts Himself to the needs and possibilities of His children. Now if God, through Our Lady, had asked us to go to Mass and receive Holy Communion every day, there would undoubtedly have been a great many people who would have said, quite rightly, that this was not possible. Some, on account of the distance separating them from the nearest Church where Mass was celebrated; others on account of the circumstances of their lives, their state in life, their job, the state of their health, etc.[225]

Lucia goes on to say, "On the other hand, to pray the Rosary is something everybody can do, rich and poor, wise and ignorant, great and small." The Rosary request keeps everyone in the loop. Anyone can pray the Rosary anywhere, whenever they are able.

"All people of good will can and must say the Rosary every day," Lucia counsels. "Why? In order to put ourselves in contact with God, to thank Him for His benefits and ask for the graces we need. It is the prayer which places us in familiar contact with God, like the son who goes to his father to thank him for the

---

[224] *"Calls,"* 131–132.
[225] Ibid., 132.

gifts he has received, to talk to him about special concerns, to receive his guidance, his help, his support and his blessing."[226]

Pointing out that we all need to pray every day, Lucia says that God asks us for "a prayer which is within our reach: the Rosary, which can be recited either in common or in private, either in church in the presence of the Blessed Sacrament or at home, either when traveling or while walking quietly in the fields." She explains, "A mother of a family can say the Rosary while she rocks her baby's cradle or does the house work. Our day has 24 hours in it. It is not asking a great deal to set aside a quarter of an hour for the spiritual life, for our intimate and familiar converse with God."

Lucia describes how she believes that, besides the Holy Mass, the Rosary—taking into account its origin, the prayers in it, and the mysteries of Redemption we recall and meditate on for each decade—"is the most pleasing prayer we can offer to God and one which is most advantageous to our own souls. If such were not the case, Our Lady would not have asked for it so insistently."[227]

Lucia also answers any questions people might have about the need for a fixed number of prayers in the Rosary, clarifying that "we need to count, in order to have a clear and vivid idea of what we are doing and to know positively whether or not we have completed what we had planned to offer to God each day, in order to preserve and enhance our relationship of intimacy with God and, by this means, preserve and enhance in ourselves our faith, hope, and charity."

And what of those people who are able to attend Mass daily? Should they still pray the Rosary daily? Of course. For all the

[226] Ibid.
[227] Ibid.

same reasons, Lucia says, "even those people who are able to assist at Mass every day should not ... neglect to say their daily Rosary." She adds this detail: "Obviously, the time they devote to saying the Rosary is not the same as that during which they are assisting at Mass. For such people, praying the Rosary can be looked upon as a way of preparing themselves to participate better in the Eucharist or as a thanksgiving after it."[228]

Moreover, Lucia describes how she sees very few truly contemplative souls who maintain within themselves "a relationship of intimate familiarity with God which prepares them for the worthy reception of Christ in the Eucharist." So vocal prayer is "necessary for them, too, meditated, pondered, and reflected upon as much as possible, as the Rosary should be."[229]

While many fine prayers can be used to prepare to receive Jesus in the Eucharist and to preserve our intimate relationship with God, Lucia notes, "I do not think that we shall find one more suited to people in general than the praying of the five or fifteen mysteries of the Rosary." She also calls the prayer of the Liturgy of the Hours marvelous, but she thinks it is not accessible to everyone.

"Perhaps for all these reasons, and others that we are unaware of," Lucia writes, "God, who is our Father and understands better than we do the needs of His children, chose to stoop to the simple ordinary level of all of us in asking for the daily recitation of the Rosary in order to smooth for us the way to Him."[230] Moreover, she says that because the Rosary is "what God through the Message, has asked us for so insistently, we can conclude that the

---

[228] Ibid., 133.
[229] Ibid.
[230] Ibid.

Rosary is the form of vocal prayer which is most suited to people in general, which we must appreciate, and which we must make every effort never to abandon."

Sister Lucia articulates the power and necessity of the Rosary beautifully when she says:

> Even for those people who do not know how, or who are not able to recollect themselves sufficiently to meditate, the simple act of taking the Rosary in their hands in order to pray is already to become mindful of God, and a mention in each decade of a mystery of the life of Christ recalls Him to their minds; this in turn will light in their souls a gentle light of faith which supports the still smoldering wick, preventing it from extinguishing itself altogether.

So what can happen if we neglect this directive from our heavenly Mother at Fatima?

Sister Lucia doesn't mince words: "Those who give up saying the Rosary and who do not go to daily Mass have nothing to sustain them, and so end up by losing themselves in the materialism of earthly life."[231]

She concludes, "Thus, the Rosary is the prayer which God, through His Church and Our Lady, has recommended most insistently to us all as a road to and a gateway of salvation: 'Pray the Rosary every day.'"

John Paul II did. Because he is so closely connected with Fatima, we need to take a look at highlights of his words of advice and wisdom concerning the Rosary. He gave them to the world in 2002 in his apostolic letter *Rosarium Virginis Mariae*. "The Rosary, though clearly Marian in character, is at heart a Christocentric

---

[231] Ibid.

prayer," the saintly Holy Father explained. "It has all the *depth of the Gospel message in its entirety*, of which it can be said to be a compendium."[232] As a side note, he credited the description of the Rosary as a "compendium" to Pope Paul VI, in his *Marialis Cultus*; Pope Paul VI, in turn, gave credit to Venerable Pius XII, who wrote in an official letter to the archbishop of Manila in 1946 that the Rosary is "the compendium of the entire Gospel."

In every part, the Rosary is as deep as the gospel message, according to John Paul II. He continued in his apostolic letter to say that the Rosary places us in "the school of Mary," who leads us to contemplate "the beauty on the face of Christ and to experience the depths of his love." By praying the Rosary, he says, we can expect to "receive abundant grace, as though from the very hands of the Mother of the Redeemer."[233]

So far, taken together, these wise insights explain why John Paul II then wrote, "The Rosary is my favorite prayer. A marvelous prayer! Marvelous in its simplicity and its depth. To recite the Rosary is nothing other than to *contemplate with Mary the face of Christ*."[234]

The Rosary should be our favorite prayer too.

John Paul II also emphasizes the Rosary as being a prayer for peace and for the family. See the Fatima connection here? Take the July 13 apparition, when Our Lady told the seers, "Continue to say the Rosary every day in honor of Our Lady of the Rosary to obtain the peace of the world and the end of the war, because

---

[232] John Paul II, Apostolic Letter *Rosarium Virginis Mariae* (October 16, 2002), no. 1.

[233] Ibid.

[234] John Paul II, *Angelus* (October 29, 1978).

only she can obtain it." God puts the peace of the world into Mary's hands, and she wants and needs our cooperation.

The Holy Father then gets right to the point about the family because of critical issues at that time concerning the family, which only heightened after 2002. He points out that "the family, the primary cell of society, [is] increasingly menaced by forces of disintegration on both the ideological and practical planes, so as to make us fear for the future of this fundamental and indispensable institution and, with it, for the future of society as a whole."[235]

The remedy he proposes: "The revival of the Rosary in Christian families, within the context of a broader pastoral ministry to the family, will be an effective aid to countering the devastating effects of this crisis typical of our age."[236] The pope also counseled that it is "beautiful and fruitful to entrust to [the Rosary] *the growth and development of children*."[237]

John Paul II next focuses on the perilous conditions of the world. He writes with great concern, "The grave challenges confronting the world at the start of this new millennium lead us to think that only an intervention from on high, capable of guiding the hearts of those living in situations of conflict and those governing the destinies of nations, can give reason to hope for a brighter future."

But echoing Our Lady's messages to us at Fatima, John Paul II states:

> *The Rosary is by its nature a prayer for peace*, since it consists in the contemplation of Christ, the Prince of Peace, the one who is "our peace" (Eph. 2:14). Anyone who

---

[235] John Paul II, *Rosarium Virginis Mariae*, no. 6.
[236] Ibid.
[237] Ibid., no. 42.

assimilates the mystery of Christ—and this is clearly the goal of the Rosary—learns the secret of peace and makes it his life's project.[238]

That peace starts with individuals. As we meditate on each mystery along with the "tranquil succession of Hail Marys, the Rosary has a peaceful effect on those who pray it."[239] It's the gift of peace that the Risen Jesus gives.

Finally, John Paul II returns to a favorite subject, and a most vital one: the family, stressing that "the Rosary is also, and always has been, *a prayer of and for the family.*"[240]

In the past, many families prayed it together. In some areas, the Rosary was a nightly staple on radio as the family gathered around to pray along. EWTN televises the Rosary daily.

A family can easily gather around a statue of our Blessed Mother or of the Holy Family, light a candle, and pray the Rosary together.

John Paul II said the family Rosary need not be a relic of the past, and it's necessary for us not to "lose this precious inheritance. We need to return to the practice of family prayer and prayer for families, continuing to use the Rosary." He also quotes Father Patrick Peyton, the Rosary priest, whose slogan, known by millions, was: "The family that prays together stays together."

"The Holy Rosary," John Paul II reaffirms, "by age-old tradition, has shown itself particularly effective as a prayer which brings the family together."[241]

---

[238] Ibid., no. 40.
[239] Ibid.
[240] Ibid., no. 41.
[241] Ibid.

And what strong plea does he end with for everyone, naming all groups from the sick and elderly to the youth? He tells every one of them, "*Confidently take up the Rosary once again*. Rediscover the Rosary in the light of Scripture, in harmony with the Liturgy, and in the context of your daily lives."[242]

The Fatima message both anchors and echoes every line that John Paul II gives to us. So how would we think of saying no to our heavenly Mother's request to pray the Rosary? The same goes for her next request.

---

[242] Ibid., no. 43.

9

Fatima's Lessons on Sacrifice

Another of Our Lady of Fatima's messages, in addition to the one about the daily Rosary, tends to be passed over by many. It is the request for sacrifice. In her book *"Calls" from the Message of Fatima*, Sister Lucia explains sacrifice, which she names "The Seventh Call of the Message."

In today's world, many people want to hear what Lucia has to say concerning sacrifice. Yet many others walk around with their hands tightly covering their ears, figuratively speaking, whenever the word "sacrifice" comes up. Our Lady spoke about it at Fatima. But if we uncover our ears and listen a bit, we will find out that making sacrifices might be easier than we think.

Looking back over her years as a Carmelite, Lucia reminds us that we're called to "offer prayers and sacrifices constantly to the Most High." She then calls us to listen to the message that calls us to "make of everything you can a sacrifice, and offer it to God as an act of reparation for the sins by which He is offended and in supplication for the conversion of sinners."[243] This was the direction given by the angel who visited the children to prepare them for Our Lady's appearance.

[243] *"Calls,"* 90.

The Fruits of Fatima

Let's also recall that, the following year, during her July 13 apparition, Our Lady told the children, "Make sacrifices for sinners, and say often, especially while making a sacrifice: 'O Jesus, this is for love of Thee, for the conversion of sinners, and in reparation for offenses committed against the Immaculate Heart of Mary.'" Lucia lays this foundation. Then she gets into specifics.

First, she reminds us that the sacrifices can be physical, spiritual, material, intellectual, or moral undertakings. We've got to be ready to take advantage of all the opportunities we see before us. We should be particularly ready to make sacrifices, she tells us, "when this is required of us in order to fulfill our duty to God, to our neighbor, and to ourselves." This counsel she gives goes right back to her second memoir, which she wrote in the first half of the twentieth century.

She told Bishop Correia da Silva: "The good Lord Himself ... bitterly and painfully complains about the extremely limited number of souls in grace who are willing to resign themselves to what is required of them in observance of his law."

"Many persons," Sr. Lucia explained, "feeling that the word penance implies great austerities, and not feeling that they have the strength for great sacrifices, become discouraged and continue a life of lukewarmness and sin." Then she said that Our Lord explained to her:

> The sacrifice that all people have to impose upon themselves is to lead a life of righteousness in the observance of His law ... because many judge the meaning of the word penance in great austerity, they do not feel the strength and pleasure to do it and are discouraged in a life of weakness and sin.

Our Lord said to me, "The sacrifice required of every person is the fulfillment of his duties in life and the observance of my Law. This is the penance that I now seek and require."[244]

That's very important. Let's stop and read it again. And again. And once more.

Now we can continue, but never forget the words of Our Lord that we've just read.

Lucia then reminds us that sacrifice is all the more necessary so that we may avoid transgressing God's commandments, to avoid sin. "Renouncing anything which might cause us to sin is the way to salvation," she directs.[245]

One of our sacrifices, Lucia tells us, will at times be "the cross of our daily work." We can see how that might be the case when our work seems repetitious and monotonous. Just think how St. Joseph had to plane a piece of wood many times to get it just right and perfectly shaped. Just think how many times Our Lady cooked meals for the Holy Family without the convenience of an electric or gas range, or how many times she went to the well to haul water back to their Nazareth home.

Such are the "difficulties of life, which occur at every step we take, and which we must accept with serenity, patience and resignation," Lucia says. "At yet other times, it will be the humiliations which happen all of a sudden and which we must accept, with confidence in God, who always helps souls who mean to raise themselves up to a better and more perfect life."[246]

When you have to wait in a long line, whether at the grocery store or the post office or elsewhere, instead of fidgeting and

[244] Ibid., 231–232.
[245] Ibid., 102.
[246] Ibid., 102–103.

being impatient, how about offering up the waiting in a spirit of sacrifice, as we're asked to do? Do it a few times, and it will start to come naturally, and some of that grace will go toward reparation for sins or to help someone struggling with sin. Our Lady knows perfectly well where and how to use that sacrifice.

In a conversation with Sister Lucia, John Haffert asked her what is meant by sacrifice. She answered, "By 'sacrifice' Our Lady said that she meant the faithful fulfillment of one's daily duty." But what about the importance of the Rosary, he asked? Lucia said that it was important "because we must pray if we are to be able to fulfill our daily duty." He then asked about the importance of the First Saturdays devotion. Again, Lucia explained, "I would say that the first Saturdays are important because, if people make them, they will purge themselves of sin once a month and renew their purpose to fulfill [their] daily duty."[247]

Finally, Haffert asked about the importance of going to the shrine at Fatima. At this point, we can surmise what Sister Lucia's answer would be. She said, "We will do far better to fulfill our daily duty."

Furthermore, Jesus had told Sister Lucia the same. Remember that the Lord had told Lucia: "The sacrifice of each one required is the fulfillment of their own duty and observance of my Law; it is penance that is now demanded and asked."[248] Can the answer to the meaning of sacrifice be any clearer?

Lucia also reminds us of the sacrifice prayer taught by Our Lady at Fatima and suggests that we add the following Morning Offering to our daily prayers because through it we offer to God all that we will do and go through in the day:

[247] Haffert, *Russia Will Be Converted*, 181, 184.
[248] *"Calls,"* 231–232.

O Jesus, through the Immaculate Heart of Mary, I offer You my prayers, works, joys, and sufferings of this day in union with the Holy Sacrifice of the Mass throughout the world. I offer them for all the intentions of Your Sacred Heart: the salvation of souls, reparation for sin, and the reunion of all Christians. I offer them for the intentions of our bishops and of all Apostles of Prayer, and in particular for those recommended by our Holy Father this month.

Doctor of the Church St. Thérèse of Lisieux taught that little sacrifices, the tiniest ones that seem not to matter or that appear inconsequential, indeed, have a great impact—sacrifices such as picking up a piece of paper off the floor.

Every day, we come across opportunities to make small sacrifices. Lucia uses the example of food and drink:

> God, like the good Father that He is, has placed such a wide variety of good and delightful things in the world which His children may, and must use as their food and even take delight in, but always in accordance with the Law of God and without forgetting to practice self-denial and moderation, which we must offer to God in thanksgiving for so many benefits and also for the benefit of our brothers and sisters in need.[249]

Moderation is the answer and antidote.

We must also strive to avoid "gluttony" of goods. Plenty of material things vie for our attention in our culture, far more so than when Sister Lucia was writing.

---

[249] Ibid., 104.

To counter wrong notions about the size of the sacrifices we ought to make, Lucia gives this explanation:

> The fact that they are small in themselves does not make them any less pleasing to God and also very meritorious and advantages to ourselves, because by means of them we prove the delicacy of our fidelity and our love for God and for our neighbor. Making such little sacrifices enriches us with grace, strengthens us in faith and charity, ennobles us before God and our neighbor, and frees us from the temptation to egoism, covetousness, envy, and self-indulgence.[250]

This explanation echoes the example of sacrifice given to us by St. Thérèse.

Lucia captures the concept in this truism: it is generosity in ordinary little things that are constantly happening; it is making perfect the present moment. See how that applies to our daily duties, too?

Lucia suggests some areas in which we can begin making sacrifices. In some cases, we don't think of them as sacrifices, or it may not be apparent how they combine with our daily duties in some instances. But let's take a look at what they are and how Lucia explains them.

Prayer
No matter where we are, God is everywhere. He listens to our praise, thanksgiving, contrition, and petitions.

We must pray with faith and attention, avoiding distraction as much as possible and keeping in mind that we're speaking to

[250] Ibid., 106.

God. We must pray with confidence and love. Why? "Because we are all in the presence of someone who we know loves us and wants to help us, like a father who takes his small son's hand in order to help him to walk: in God's eyes we are always small fragile children who are weak in the practice of virtue, who are constantly tripping and falling, which is why we need our Father to give us His hand to help keep us on our feet and walking in the ways of holiness."[251]

This can often mean a sacrifice of our own likes, such as sacrificing "a little of our time for relaxation," Lucia said.[252] Maybe we have to get up a little earlier in the morning so we can attend Mass. Or, before going to bed at night, we can turn off the TV or the radio and pray the Rosary, or set aside another time to pray the Rosary.

Food and Drink

Lucia counsels us to "offer to God the sacrifice of some little act of self-denial in the matter of food, but not to the extent of impairing the physical strength we need in order to do our work."[253]

She offers a couple of tips. Choose a fruit, dessert, or drink that you don't particularly like instead of one that's on your usual "like" list. Put up with thirst for a little while before taking a drink, and then make it one of those you don't especially like. Abstain from alcohol, or avoid drinking it to excess. When serving yourself at a meal, don't take the best.

Lest we become Pharisees blowing our own horns in the marketplace, Lucia adds this caution for us when making such

---

[251] Ibid.
[252] Ibid.
[253] Ibid., 107.

sacrifices. If we can't avoid abstaining from food or drink without drawing attention to ourselves, we should

> take it with simplicity and without scruple, thanking God for spoiling us.... God created good things for His children and likes to see us making use of them, without abusing them, and then fulfilling our duty of working to deserve them, and making use of them with gratitude and love for the One who heaps gifts upon us.

Clothing

Lucia begins with an unexpected take on sacrifice in terms of clothing, which she said we not only can but must make: put up with a little heat or cold without complaining. If other people are in the room with us, let them open or close windows and doors as they want to.

Next, dress modestly and decently without becoming a slave to the latest fashions. Refrain from adopting fashion when it doesn't align with or agree with these two virtues of modestly and decency. This is very important, Lucia explains, "so that we ourselves may not be, by our way of dressing, a cause of sin for others, bearing in mind that we are responsible for the sins that others commit because of us." To avoid the temptation of fashions, we must be cautious about what we see on television, in movies, in ads, in magazines, and so forth.

Remember that it was revealed to Jacinta when she was in the Lisbon orphanage for sick children that "fashions will much offend our Lord. People who serve God should not follow the fashions. The Church has no fashions. Our Lord is always the same."[254]

---

[254] De Marchi, *True Story*, 158.

Lucia makes clear that "we must dress in accordance with Christian morals, personal dignity, and solidarity with others, offering to God the sacrifice of exaggerated vanity."[255] She suggests refraining from buying loads of jewelry and using the money to help those in need. We can also opt for simple, less costly clothes over expensive attire.

Behavior
Other people give us ample opportunities to make sacrifices. But don't complain. Put up with little annoyances you come across on your daily path. Maybe it's an unpleasant word spoken to you or one that's irritating or downright disagreeable. Maybe it's a scornful glare. Or maybe it's being passed over, ignored, or forgotten. Maybe it's a rejection. Maybe it's ingratitude.

Let them drop, says Lucia. Offer them to God as sacrifices. We must let these things pass "as if we were blind, deaf, and dumb, so that we may in fact see better, speak with greater certainty, and hear the voice of God." Let others "seem to have their way." Lucia says "seem" because "in reality the one who prevails is the one who knows how to keep silent for the love of God. Cheerfully to allow others to occupy the first places, whatever is best for them, let them enjoy and take credit for the fruit of our labors, of our sacrifices, of our activities, of our ability, of things that have been taken from us."[256]

Then Lucia with yet more clear guidance prompts us to go one step further in sacrifice. She encourages us to "endure with a good grace the company of those we do not like or whom we find

---

[255] "*Calls,*" 107.
[256] Ibid. 108.

disagreeable, of those who go against us, upset us, and torment us with indiscreet or even unkind questions."

How should we react to these people? "Let us repay them with a smile, a little kind deed done for them, a favor forgiving and loving, with our eyes fixed on God," Lucia writes. She goes on to say, "This denial of ourselves is often the most difficult for our human nature, but it is also the one most pleasing to God and meritorious for ourselves."[257] Didn't St. Paul say the same in the passage we all know from 1 Corinthians 13, explaining that love is patient, kind, not pompous, not inflated, not rude, does not seek its own interests, is not quick-tempered, does not brood over injury, and endures all things?

By meeting God in prayer, we gain the grace and the strength needed to make the sacrifices required of us in our daily lives. And in making these sacrifices, we fulfill the Fatima request to "make of everything you can a sacrifice and offer it to God as an act of reparation for the sins by which He is offended and in supplication for the conversion of sinners." As we offer these things day by day, notice how our sacrifices lead to some gifts for us too. Gluttony gives way to moderation and temperance. We advance in modesty, patience, perseverance, humility, endurance, hope, and charity. And the list of virtues grows.

As Sister Lucia recommended, praying the Morning Offering when we wake up is a perfect way to make sure we're offering everything up in case we forget to mention something during the day.

[257] Ibid.

10

The Distinctive Days That Highlight Fatima

Heaven can highlight the messages of major events and apparitions in many ways. One way of highlighting them may even be the specific days of the week on which these events take place. Could this be the case with Fatima, since several major events took place on Saturdays and Thursdays? Might Fatima's message echo even today on Saturdays and Thursdays? The evidence seems too obviously providential.

First and always, remember that the messages and directions from Our Lady of Fatima are essential and indispensable in order to bring peace to the world. The Miracle of the Sun and its anniversary reminders broadcast that truth to us loud and clear.

But how do Saturdays and Thursdays fit into the Fatima picture? What might they tell us?

To begin, recall that the significance of certain months also plays a role. The Church dedicates May to the Blessed Virgin Mary. Mary appeared for the first time at Fatima in May.

Then came October, the month of the Holy Rosary. On October 13 at Fatima, Our Lady identified herself: "I am the Lady of the Rosary." At that time, she again called for the daily Rosary.

The Fruits of Fatima

Before we get into the significance of Saturdays and Thursdays, let's look at a vital detail and recall one more little-realized fact that accentuates Fatima's message. Although Our Lady's first appearance on May 13 was not on a Saturday but a Sunday, that *date* was the liturgical feast of Our Lady of the Eucharist (also sometimes known as Our Lady of the Blessed Sacrament).

The late Father Robert Fox, the founder of the Fatima Family Apostolate International, who regularly assisted at the Shrine of the Most Blessed Sacrament in Hanceville, Alabama, made note of this fact. He said, "When our Blessed Mother came to Fatima, she came as Our Lady of Peace — all of Light — and she came as Our Lady of the Holy Eucharist."

And who originally gave her that title joining her with the Eucharist? As we've seen, it was St. Peter Julian Eymard, who was called "the Priest of the Eucharist" and "the Apostle of the Eucharist." It was in May 1868. He founded the Congregation of the Most Blessed Sacrament, which was approved on May 13, 1856.

Now, then, let's discuss Saturday's significance.

We know that the Church devotes Saturdays to the Blessed Mother. It's her special day. Many major Marian events throughout the centuries have happened on Saturdays. It's as if they were a prelude to the main event of Fatima. Let's consider just a few before we look at the Fatima connection.

Saturday, November 27, 1830, was the day before Advent began that year. That Saturday, our Blessed Mother appeared to St. Catherine Labouré in the chapel of the motherhouse of the Daughters of Charity in Paris to give her the Miraculous Medal. Describing the design, Our Lady said the medal was to have the inscription, "O Mary, conceived without sin, pray for us who have recourse to thee." The medal was to be spread far and wide — it was, and it continues to be spread today.

Saturday, September 19, 1846, was the day Mary appeared as Our Lady of La Salette to the young Melanie Calvat and Maximum Giraud with an important message about amending lifestyles and turning back to God.

On Saturday, December 9, 1531, Our Lady of Guadalupe appeared for the first time to St. Juan Diego. (The Julian calendar was still in use at that time.) She told him, "Because truly I am your compassionate Mother, yours and that of all the people that live together in this land, and also of all the other various lineages of men, those who love me, those who cry to me, those who seek me, those who trust in me."[258]

Looking at just these major apparitions, we can see that Saturday is surely Mary's day. But let's go back centuries further. In the early days of the Church, Christians had already begun the practice of honoring Mary on Saturdays. As Sunday was the Lord's Day, Saturday soon became Mary's day.

In a great talk given in 1947 on Our Lady of Fatima, Servant of God Father John Hardon gave a clear picture of the history of Saturday as the day dedicated to Mary and Marian devotion from the Church's first centuries. For one, St. Innocent I, who reigned from 401 to 417, wrote the faithful a significant letter decreeing that each Saturday was to be observed as a day of abstinence in honor of the Sorrows of the Blessed Virgin Mary.

Skipping to the eighth century, St. John of Damascus made known that Saturdays were dedicated to Mary in the Church of the East and celebrated as such. Saturday Masses in honor of Mary are found in ninth- and tenth-century liturgical books.

---

[258] Carl Anderson and Msgr. Eduardo Chavez, *Our Lady of Guadalupe: Mother of the Civilization of Love* (New York: Doubleday, 2009), 9.

Sts. Bernard, Bonaventure, and Thomas Aquinas explained that Mary is honored on Saturdays because, while Christ was in the tomb and others had abandoned Him, it was only Mary who continued to believe and await His rising from the dead, as He had promised.

St. Bernard firmly states, "In Mary alone did the faith of the Church remain steadfast during the three days that Jesus lay in the tomb. And although everyone else wavered, she who conceived Christ in faith, kept the faith that she had once for all received from God and never lost. Thus, could she wait with assured hope for the glory of the Risen Lord."[259]

The saints certainly substantiate Saturday as Mary's day. As if to prophesy the apparitions of Our Lady at Fatima and elsewhere, much as the Old Testament prophets spoke of what was to come, in the twelfth century St. Bernard of Clairvaux, a major Marian devotee, preached:

> In dangers, in doubts, in difficulties, think of Mary, call upon Mary. Let not her name depart from your lips, never suffer it to leave your heart. And that you may obtain the assistance of her prayer, neglect not to walk in her footsteps. With her for guide, you shall never go astray; while invoking her, you shall never lose heart; so long as she is in your mind, you are safe from deception; while she holds your hand, you cannot fall; under her protection you have nothing to fear; if she walks before you, you shall not grow weary; if she shows you favor, you shall reach the goal.

[259] Father John Hardon, "Our Lady of Fatima in the Light of History," *Review for Religious* 6 (May 1947), Real Presence Association, www.therealpresence.org/archives/Mariology/Mariology_030.htm.

That surely fits the image of Mary we get at Fatima, too, does it not?

St. Thomas Aquinas gave his interpretation of the connection between Mary and Saturday, saying, "Since the Resurrection took place on a Sunday, we keep holy this day instead of the Sabbath, as did the Jews of old. However, we also sanctify Saturday in honor of the glorious Virgin Mary, who remained unshaken in faith all day Saturday after the death of her Divine Son."[260]

In the sixteenth century, St. Charles Borromeo prayed the Rosary and Our Lady's Office every day on his knees. Father Hardon describes the saint:

> On hearing the Angelus bell, though the ground might be wet and muddy, he would fall on his knees even in the public street. Over the main door of every church in the archdiocese, he caused an image of Mary to be placed as a reminder to the faithful that she is the Gate of Heaven.... St. Alphonsus Liguori records of him that he fasted on bread and water every Saturday of the year in praise of the Mother of God.[261]

St. Charles Borromeo died on November 3, 1584, a Saturday.

Father Hardon noted that in the eighteenth century, St. Alphonsus Liguori wrote:

> It is well known that Saturday has been set aside by the Church as Mary's Day because it was on the Sabbath after the death of her Son that she remained unshaken in her faith. For this reason, the clients of Mary are careful to

---

[260] Ibid.
[261] Ibid.

honor her on that day by some particular devotion and especially by fasting.... I affirm that those who practice this devotion can hardly be lost; not that I mean to say that if they die in mortal sin the Blessed Virgin will deliver them, but that those who practice it will, through Mary's help, find perseverance in God's grace easy and obtain from her a happy death.... On Saturdays we should always practice some devotion in honor of Our Blessed Lady, receive Holy Communion, or hear Mass, visit an image of Mary, or something of that sort.[262]

Now for the Fatima-Saturday connection.

October 13, 1917, the day the big miracle occurred at Fatima —the Miracle of the Sun—was a Saturday. It was Mary's special day, the day of the week the Church dedicates to Mary, this time in more ways than one. Our Lady identified herself and called again for people to pray the Rosary and to stop offending God. She also appeared under three of her titles. And the Holy Family appeared. Many lessons and requests are summarized in that apparition.

On Saturday, December 17, 1927, Sister Lucia had a vision of Jesus. In Pontevedra, Spain, she went before the Blessed Sacrament in the tabernacle because she wanted heaven's permission to reveal part of the secret that her spiritual director asked her to include in her memoirs. She asked Jesus "how she should comply with what had been asked of her, that is, to say if the origin of the devotion to the Immaculate Heart of Mary was included in the Secret that the most holy Virgin had confided to her."[263]

---

[262] Ibid.
[263] *Memoirs*, 193.

Lucia tells of what happened next in the third person: "Jesus made her hear very distinctly these words: 'My daughter, write what they ask of you. Write also all that the most holy Virgin revealed to you in the Apparition, in which she spoke of this devotion. As for the remainder of the Secret, continue to keep silence.'"[264]

What was Lucia referring to that she was asked to reveal? It was about the major part of the Fatima message, calling for devotion to the Immaculate Heart of Mary. Lucia wrote that in 1917, Our Lady said, "Jesus wishes to make use of you to make me known and loved. He wants to establish in the world devotion to my Immaculate Heart. I promise salvation to those who embrace it, and these souls will be loved by God, like flowers placed by me to adorn His throne."[265] There's the all-important devotion to the Immaculate Heart of Mary that Jesus tells her to reveal.

Finally, the most obvious Fatima-Saturday connection is that of the Five First Saturdays devotion. Remember, this devotion requires receiving Holy Communion and praying the Rosary, which Our Lady asked everyone to pray during each of her apparitions. The Eucharist is clearly a major part of Fatima along with the Rosary and devotion to the Immaculate Heart of Mary.

These connections proclaim the divine import of Our Lady's requests and promises.

What might the Fatima-Thursday significance be?

Thursday is traditionally the day of the week on which we remember the Holy Eucharist, because Jesus instituted the Eucharist on a Thursday, at the Last Supper.

---

[264] Ibid., 193–194.
[265] Ibid., 194.

The Fruits of Fatima

On Thursday, December 10, 1925, the Blessed Mother appeared to Lucia. The Child Jesus stood on a luminous cloud next to His Mother. Lucia describes how Our Lady rested her hand upon Lucia's shoulder and showed her "a heart encircled by thorns, which she was holding in her other hand. At the same time, the Child said: 'Have compassion on the Heart of your most holy Mother, covered with thorns, with which ungrateful men pierce it at every moment, and there is no one to make an act of reparation to remove them.'"[266]

Although we've already read Our Lady's next words in an earlier chapter, they bear repeating. Our Lady told Lucia:

Look, my daughter, at my Heart, surrounded with thorns with which ungrateful men pierce me at every moment by their blasphemies and ingratitude. You at least try to console me and say that I promise to assist at the hour of death, with the graces necessary for salvation, all those who, on the first Saturday of five consecutive months, shall confess, receive Holy Communion, recite five decades of the Rosary, and keep me company for fifteen minutes while meditating on the fifteen mysteries of the Rosary, with the intention of making reparation to me.

Then, on Thursday, June 13, 1929, Sister Lucia, a Dorothean at the time, had yet another vision at the convent in Tuy, Spain. Again, it was a revelation of the Immaculate Heart of Mary and of the Blessed Trinity. There was a reference in the vision to the Holy Eucharist, too. It took place as Lucia was making her usual Thursday 11 p.m. Holy Hour in the chapel.

---

[266] Carmel of Coimbra, A *Pathway*, 158.

Prostrate in the middle of the chapel, with her arms forming a cross, Lucia was praying the prayers the angel had taught the seers years ago. When she stood up to continue these prayers, Lucia says, "Suddenly the whole chapel was illumined by a supernatural light and, above the altar, appeared a Cross of light reaching to the ceiling. In a brighter light on the upper part of the Cross could be seen the face of a man and His body to the waist; upon His breast was a dove also of light and nailed to the Cross was the body of another man."[267]

Notice the distinct reference to the Eucharist next. "A little below the waist I could see a chalice and a large Host suspended in the air," says Lucia, "onto which drops of blood were falling from the face of Jesus Crucified and from the wound in His side. These drops ran down onto the Host and fell into the chalice." [268]

Now comes the Fatima reference: "Beneath the right arm of the cross was Our Lady. (It was Our Lady of Fatima, with Her Immaculate Heart ... in her left hand ... without a sword or roses, but with a crown of thorns and flames....) Under the left arm of the cross were large letters, as if of crystal clear water which ran down upon the altar and formed these words: 'Grace and Mercy.'" [269]

Lucia understood this as the mystery of the Most Holy Trinity being revealed to her. Our Lady then told her about her Immaculate Heart again: "The moment has come in which God asks the Holy Father, in union with all the bishops of the world, to make the consecration of Russia to my Immaculate Heart,

---

[267] *Memoirs*, 197.
[268] Ibid.
[269] Carmel of Coimbra, *A Pathway*, 184.

promising to save it by this means. There are so many souls whom the justice of God condemns for sins committed against me that I have come to ask reparation: sacrifice yourself for this intention and pray."[270]

This extraordinary vision isn't the only Thursday connection to Fatima.

On Thursday, May 13, 1937, the apostolic nuncio went to Fatima to head the first Portuguese national pilgrimage there. Some half a million pilgrims joined him.

On Thursday, May 13, 1948, the thirty-first anniversary of Our Lady's first apparition, Sister Lucia went from the Dorothean Sisters to be received into the Order of Mount Carmel.

On Thursday, May 13, 1982, Pope John Paul II returned to Fatima for two reasons: to thank Our Lady for saving his life during the previous year's assassination attempt and to celebrate the sixty-fifth anniversary of the Fatima apparitions. He celebrated Mass, and during his homily he said, "This call was uttered at the beginning of the twentieth century, and it was thus addressed particularly to this present century. *The Lady of the message* seems to have read with special insight the 'signs of the times,' the signs of our time.... The call to repentance is a motherly one, and at the same time it is strong and decisive."

Because Our Lady's message was both urgent and prophetic for our day too, it's good to mull over more of what John Paul II had to say on the matter that day. He went on:

And so, while the message of Our Lady of Fatima is a motherly one, it is also strong and decisive. It sounds severe. It sounds like John the Baptist speaking on the

[270] Ibid.

banks of the Jordan. It invites to repentance. It gives a warning. It calls to prayer. It recommends the Rosary....

Today John Paul II ... presents himself, reading again with trepidation the motherly call to penance, to conversion, the ardent appeal of the Heart of Mary that resounded at Fatima sixty-five years ago. Yes, he reads it again with trepidation in his heart because he sees how many people and societies—how many Christians—have gone in the opposite direction to the one indicated in the message of Fatima. Sin has thus made itself firmly at home in the world, and denial of God has become widespread in the ideologies, ideas, and plans of human beings.

But for this very reason the evangelical call to repentance and conversion, uttered in the Mother's message, remains ever relevant. It is still more relevant than it was sixty-five years ago. It is still more urgent.

And this was in 1982.

Let's stop for a minute and consider that if people had listened to Our Lady's requests starting in 1917, there would have been no World War II, for a start. And how can anyone overlook the shocking deterioration of the world and culture in every aspect since the saintly John Paul II proclaimed this observation in 1982?

At the same time, John Paul II went on to say that, in the midst of all this, his heart rejoiced in hope at the consecrations of the world to the Mother because it meant consecrating the world to Jesus, Infinite Holiness:

This Holiness means redemption. It means a love more powerful than evil. No "sin of the world" can ever overcome this Love.

The Fruits of Fatima

Mary's appeal is not for just once. Her appeal must be taken up by generation after generation, in accordance with the ever new "signs of the times." It must be unceasingly returned to. It must ever be taken up anew.

Our situation in the world calls for a faithful response to Mary's requests now more than ever — Thursdays, Saturdays, every day of the week.

11

The Feast of Our Lady of Fatima
Is Truly Mother's Day

Mother's Day in the United States always finds people celebrating in a big way. Mothers are showered with gifts, and restaurants experience one of their busiest days of the year as families treat Mom to dinner. People in the United States were celebrating Mother's Day on that May 13, 1917, when our Blessed Mother first appeared at Fatima.

But that May 13 was Mother's Day in a universal way, as our heavenly Mother came to bring peace to families, to countries, to the world—to give us her motherly message that we must cease offending our Father and live by His laws.

On May 13, 1967, the fiftieth anniversary of Fatima—a Saturday, and the eve of Mother's Day—Pope St. Paul VI released his apostolic exhortation *Signum Magnum*, reminding us that Mary is Mother of Christ, Mother of the Church, and that she "continues to fulfill from heaven her maternal function as the cooperator in the birth and development of divine life in the individual souls of redeemed men." Simply put, she's our Mother, our spiritual heavenly Mother.

Was it a coincidence that Fatima's anniversary and Mother's Day fell on the same day? What a providential connection there appears to be between Mary's motherly concern for us and honoring our Mother!

Don't we honor our mothers on Mother's Day because they want the best for us? Hopefully that means that they strive for our salvation, first and foremost. Our Mother Mary certainly strives for the salvation of all her children. Fatima is perfect proof. At Fatima, our Blessed Mother shows herself a mother who guides and teaches her children the path to God.

In *Signum Magnum*, Pope Paul VI wrote specifically about our Mother's influence through example and how we should follow it. He said that just as parents' teachings become stronger by their example, "the immaculate Mother of God attracts souls in an irresistible way to imitation of the divine model, Jesus Christ, of whom she was the most faithful image."

He affirmed, "It is therefore the duty of all Christians to imitate in a reverent spirit the examples of goodness left to them by their heavenly Mother.... It is, in fact, a natural thing that the children should have the same sentiments of their mothers and should reflect their merits and virtues."

The wisdom in Paul VI's words is quite evident. If earthly mothers want their children to be good, how much more does our heavenly Mother want us to be good? We do that by listening to her and imitating her. She made it simple at Fatima.

Don't we also honor our mothers for the counsel they gave us, advising us on which pursuits may be beneficial to us and which would likely lead us into danger or even ruin? Didn't our Blessed Mother in her apparitions at Fatima make it very clear to the children, and to us her children, the spiritual disasters, not to mention the temporal ones, resulting from following the ways of the world?

Did we listen to our mothers when they cautioned us to put those matches down so we wouldn't get burned? Sure, we did. But not enough of us listened to our heavenly Mother on Mother's Day, May 13, 1917, and later that summer when she said, "If you do what I tell you, many souls will be saved, and there will be peace. This war will end, but if men do not refrain from offending God, another and more terrible war will begin."

One look at the history of the twentieth century and today's secular society tells us that most of our Mother's children have not listened but remain disobedient and have become further corrupted.

When we honor our mothers on Mother's Day, do we think of the times they helped us with our bruises and hurts? And doesn't a mother comfort her child who calls in the middle of the night after waking from a nightmare? Our heavenly Mother will do the same if we call to her and listen to her advice to quell the nightmarish attacks upon all that is good in this world. The tiniest whisper to her will have her by our side to help.

We know that two dreadful "nightmares" surround the degradation of motherhood and marriage. In 1981, Sister Lucia wrote to Cardinal Carlo Caffarra, who, in a 2008 interview, revealed, "In that letter we find written, 'The final battle between the Lord and the kingdom of Satan will be about marriage and the family.' Don't be afraid, she added, because whoever works for the sanctity of marriage and the family will always be fought against and opposed in every way, because this is the decisive issue. Then she concluded, 'Nevertheless, Our Lady has already crushed his head.'"

Our Mother Mary prayerfully intercedes for us, her children, and gave us the remedy back in 1917 to extinguish these "nightmares." John Paul II pointed to that remedy again in his homily in Fatima 1982, when he said, "The call to repentance is linked, as always, with a call to prayer.... The Lady of the message indicates the Rosary, which can rightly be defined as 'Mary's prayer': the prayer in which she feels particularly united with us. She herself prays with us."

Good mothers keep after their children to get them on the right path. Our Blessed Mother certainly does. In each appearance, she reminded us, "Continue to say the Rosary every day in honor of Our Lady of the Rosary to obtain the peace of the world and the end of the war, because only she can obtain it." Again, she would repeat herself, saying, "I want you to continue saying the Rosary every day."

At Fatima, on May 13, 1982, John Paul II reminded us of Our Lady's motherly love: "In the words of Fatima, we seem to find this dimension of motherly love, whose range covers the whole of man's path towards God. The solicitude of the Mother of the Savior is solicitude for the work of salvation: the work of her Son. It is solicitude for the salvation, the eternal salvation, of all."

A mother never gives up on her children. "In the light of a mother's love we understand the whole message of the Lady of Fatima," John Paul II noted. "She not only calls us to be converted: she calls us to accept her motherly help to return to the source of Redemption."

The motherly directions of Our Lady of Fatima are as crucial as ever. As her children we're called to follow them. We have to ask ourselves: Do we honor our mothers only on Mother's Day? The answer should be, "Of course not." What better way to honor our Blessed Mother and make every single day of the year Mother's Day for her than by following the counsel and requests of Our Lady of Fatima?

12

Holy Fathers Hail Fatima

It's significant that the Church is a major promoter of Fatima. Holy Fathers have consistently encouraged us, with their words and devotion, to embrace the Fatima message.

"We would be mistaken to think that Fatima's prophetic mission is complete," said Pope Benedict XVI in 2010, when he celebrated Mass in Fatima to mark the tenth anniversary of the beatification of Jacinta and Francisco Marto.

But Benedict and John Paul II, whose constant devotion to Fatima is well known, aren't the first popes to be dedicated to Fatima. From the start, Holy Fathers have had their eyes fixed on what happened there and its importance for the world.

Once the major apparitions concluded on October 13, it was up to the local bishop to investigate and give first approval. After much study, the proclamation by the bishop of Leiria-Fatima declaring the apparitions authentic and supernatural came on October 13, 1930, exactly thirteen years after the final apparition and the Miracle of the Sun. It was quite providential, since every visit of the Blessed Mother in 1917 was scheduled for the thirteenth of the month.

The proclamation by Bishop José Alves Correia da Silva declared the apparitions of Fatima worthy of belief and officially permitted devotion to Our Lady of Fatima. The bishop added that "it is a great reason for joy and consolation, this grace that the Most Holy Virgin has granted us; greater is the obligation on us to correspond with Her goodness."[271] At the same time, he recommended

> in a special manner, affection for Our Lord in the Blessed Sacrament, devotion to the Most Holy Virgin, to St. Joseph, to the holy souls in purgatory, to the daily recitation of at least five decades of the Rosary, avoidance of sins of the flesh, of immodest attire and immoral readings; the practice of penance, which Jesus so much insisted on, and the Virgin, Our Lady recalled so much to mind; charity towards all our brethren and principally towards the sick and the poor.[272]

The bishop's declaration came during the reign of Pius XI. This pope figured into the apparition of July 13, 1917, during which Our Lady gave the children a vision of hell. She told the children that World War I was going to end. "But if people do not cease offending God," she said, "a worse one will break out during the pontificate of Pius XI."[273]

Looking back, we know the worse war that our Blessed Mother referred to conditionally—that "if" depended upon the people's response to her request and instruction—would be World War II. But look again at what else she prophesied.

Our Lady said it would begin when Pius XI was pope. This was in 1917, when the Holy Father was still Benedict XV. This

[271] Martins, *Documents on Fatima*, 290.
[272] Ibid., 291.
[273] Apostoli, *Fatima for Today*, 71.

is very significant, looking at the date. There was no Pius XI *until five years later*—February 6, 1922.

Pius XI was pope until he died on February 10, 1939. During his reign, he fearlessly spoke out against fascism and the Nazi Reich in his encyclical *Mit Brennender Sorge*, and he pointed to the horrendous threats of religious extermination and of Communism in his encyclical *Divini Redemptoris*. Among the saints Pius XI canonized were Thomas More and Thérèse of Lisieux, whom he had also beatified. He established the feast of Christ the King. But there was no apparent move regarding the apparitions during his pontificate.

One little point bothered some people. They thought that World War II didn't begin until Pius XII was elected pope. But Lucia insisted the name given was Pius XI and that the war really began in 1938 with the occupation of Austria.

The First Fatima Pope

St. John Paul II is often called "the Fatima Pope," and rightly so. But before him, there was another often-overlooked major Marian and Fatima pope, the first Holy Father to popularize the apparitions at Fatima. He can rightly be named "the *first* Fatima Pope." And it might not be who you think.

"Fatima owes its present popularity in the Church very largely to the interest and encouragement of Pope Pius XII."[274] So wrote Servant of God Father John Hardon in 1952.

Just months after being elected pope, Pius XII approved the Fatima apparitions in 1940. Father Hardon points out that he

---

[274] Fr. John A. Hardon, S.J., "Pius XII and Our Lady," *Review for Religious* 11 (September 1952), posted at The Real Presence Association, http://www.therealpresence.org/archives/Mariology/Mariology_005.htm.

was the first Holy Father who "explicitly referred to Fatima in a formal papal document."[275] This recognition came in his encyclical *Saeculo Exeunte Octavo*, which encouraged the Church in Portugal in its missionary work, mentioning Fatima more than once. He wrote that "the faithful, when reciting the Rosary so highly commended by the Blessed Virgin at Fatima, should entreat this same Virgin to intercede in favor of this divine vocation in order that the missions will flourish."[276]

Pius XII added, "And the Blessed Virgin Mary of the Rosary, who is venerated at Fatima and is the same great Mother of God who obtained a great victory at Lepanto, will be with you with her powerful protection."[277] The Holy Father called Mary by the title that she used to identify herself during the apparition on October 13, 1917.

The encyclical, by the way, was released on June 13, 1940, the anniversary of one of the apparitions. With this revelation, it wouldn't be far afield to believe that Pius XII's link to Fatima was ordained by heaven.

And there's more. The connections date to the apparitions. "On 13 May 1917, while the Mother of God was appearing in Fatima, announcing to the world her message of peace and conversion and warning humanity about the terrible crises of the twentieth century, in the Sistine Chapel in Rome ... Eugenio Pacelli, the future Pius XII, was being consecrated Archbishop by Pope Benedict XV," Emilia Paola Pacelli writes in *L'Osservatore Romano*.[278] It bears

---

[275] Ibid.

[276] Pius XII, Encyclical *Saeculo Exeunte Octavo* (June 13, 1940), no. 17.

[277] Ibid., no. 52.

[278] Emilia Paola Pacelli, "In the Light of Fatima towards the Third Millennium: Pius XII, Father, Teacher and Friend of Our Time,"

repeating: this was *the very day* our Blessed Mother first appeared to the children at Fatima.

From his early childhood, Eugenio Pacelli, the future Pius XII, was exceptionally devoted to the Blessed Mother. "Indeed, the Blessed Virgin had taken that son by the hand when he was still very young," the *L'Osservatore Romano* article notes.

To and from school, he would stop and pray before the miraculous image of Mary in the chapel of Madonna della Strada in Rome. Ordained on Easter Sunday 1899, the future Pius XII chose to celebrate his first Mass on Easter Monday at the Basilica of Our Lady of the Snows at the altar before the image of Mary, "Salvation of the Roman People."

The connections between this Holy Father, Mary, and Fatima would continuously grow. On October 31, 1942, after receiving a letter from Sister Lucia, sent to him on the instructions of her bishop, Pius XII, speaking in Portuguese over the radio, consecrated the world to the Immaculate Heart of Mary. This was a worthy response to the desire of Our Lord, made known through Mary, that devotion to the Immaculate Heart be established in the world.

On the same day, Pius XII also made the first attempt to consecrate Russia, as Our Lady requested. Later we'll see how this consecration went and what happened as a result.

Earlier, on May 13, 1942, the Vatican had published the Message of Fatima and the first two of the three Fatima Secrets, with the Holy Father's approval. We can only wonder about his surprise to see how Our Lady's prophecy about a great war coming, beginning in the reign of Pius XI, had come to pass.

L'Osservatore Romano, August 9, 1998, www.ewtn.com/library/ CHISTORY/ORPACELI.HTM.

The Fruits of Fatima

After being elected pope in 1939, with war erupting in Europe, Pius XII at once focused on Marian devotion, writing the first of a series of May letters for Mary's month, asking Our Lady to restore peace among the nations. He wrote, "As the month of May approaches, when the faithful are accustomed to raise special prayers to the Holy Virgin, it is close to Our heart ... that during this period public prayers be offered in the dioceses and parishes in the cause (of world peace.)" He called especially for the powerful prayers of innocent children.

In his 1941 letter, Pius XII reminded that the war, with its griefs, was in great part a punishment from God for sins, and people were to seek mercy through God's Mother, Mary. Surely, he was not yet aware of what Our Lady of Fatima in 1917 had prophesied about this greater war if men did not turn from their sinful ways.

In 1943, in his encyclical *Mystici Corporis Christi*, Pius XII extolled Mary "to whose Immaculate Heart We have trustfully consecrated all mankind, and who now reigns in heaven with her Son, her body and soul refulgent with heavenly glory."

One Marian declaration after another continued. In 1944, Pius XII placed his pontificate under Our Lady's patronage and extended the feast of the Immaculate Heart to the Universal Church to be celebrated on August 22. (In 1969, Paul VI moved this feast to the Saturday after the solemnity of the Sacred Heart of Jesus.) That year, under obedience to her bishop and with the permission of the Blessed Mother, Sister Lucia wrote out the Third Secret entrusted to the visionaries, but she said it could not be opened until 1960.

In 1946, for Fatima's anniversary on May 13, Pius XII sent Cardinal Benedetto Masella to Portugal as his personal representative to preside over the canonical coronation of the image of Our Lady of Fatima. The crown on the statue now contains the bullet that wounded John Paul II during an assassination attempt and that he himself brought to Fatima in 1982 to place in the crown.

In 1948, after Sister Lucia's plea to him, Pius XII gave permission for her to join the Carmelites. She thanked him and entered the Carmel in Coimbra.

The same year, in his May encyclical *Auspicia Quaedam*, calling for prayers for world peace, Pius XII again highlighted consecration to the Immaculate Heart of the Virgin Mary: "It is our wish ... that wherever the opportunity suggests itself, this consecration be made in the various dioceses as well as in each of the parishes and families. And We are confident that abundant blessings and favors from heaven will surge forth from this private and public consecration."

On May 18, 1950, the pope again sent a message to the people of Portugal regarding Fatima: "May Portugal never forget the heavenly message of Fatima, which, before anybody else, she was blessed to hear. To keep Fatima in your heart and to translate Fatima into deeds is the best guarantee for ever more graces." In many other messages and in his encyclicals *Fulgens Corona* (1953) and *Ad Caeli Reginam* (1954), Pius XII encouraged the veneration of the Virgin in Fatima.

What's more, in 1950, Pius XII privately saw the Miracle of the Sun—the same phenomenon that had occurred on October 13, 1917—several times within days of his declaration on the dogma of the Assumption of the Blessed Virgin Mary. The dogma was officially established on November 1, 1950, showing again Pius XII's love and reverence for Mary. In *Munificentissimus Deus*, he referred to himself as "we, who have placed our pontificate under the special patronage of the most holy Virgin, to whom we have had recourse so often in times of grave trouble, we who have consecrated the entire human race to her Immaculate Heart in public ceremonies, and who have time and time again experienced her powerful protection."

Pius XII saw the Miracle of the Sun not once, not twice, but four times. "I have seen the 'Miracle of the Sun.' This is the pure truth," he wrote of events that had begun just two days before his proclamation of the dogma of the Assumption.[279]

Years later he described the events in handwritten notes. They were on public display at a Vatican exhibit in November 2008, as recorded in Catholic news. The Holy Father wrote that, at 4 p.m. on October 30, 1950, during his usual walk in the Vatican Gardens, "I was awestruck by a phenomenon that before now I had never seen. The sun, which was still quite high, looked like a pale, opaque sphere, entirely surrounded by a luminous circle," he recalled, and he could look at it "without the slightest bother. There was a very light little cloud in front of it." The Holy Father also said the sun "moved outward slightly, either spinning, or moving from left to right and vice versa."[280]

Pius XII related how he saw the same miracle again on October 31 and November 1, "the day of the definition of the dogma of the Assumption, and then again November 8, and after that, no more."[281] He took it as a divine sign endorsing the dogma's proclamation.

The dogma was proclaimed thirty-three years after the Fatima apparitions.

[279] Antonio Gaspari, "Pius XII Saw 'Miracle of the Sun.'" Zenit, November 4, 2008, https://zenit.org/articles/pius-xii-saw-miracle-of-the-sun/.

[280] Ibid.

[281] Ibid.

The October 13, 1951, celebration at Fatima drew more than a million pilgrims to the Cova. Assisting at the celebration was Cardinal Federico Tedeschini, whom Pius XII sent as his legate for this major event.

For the event, speaking over the radio, Pius XII, who was fervently devoted to the Rosary, gave pilgrims this message: "The Virgin Mother's insistence on the recitation of the family Rosary was meant to teach us that the secret of peace in family life lies in imitating the virtues of the Holy Family." This was one of countless occasions when Pius XII spoke about the Rosary.

The month before, on September 15, 1951, the feast of the Seven Sorrows of the Virgin Mary, he released his encyclical *Ingruentium Malorum*. In it, Pius XII said that ever since becoming pope, he "never ceased, in the face of approaching evils, to entrust to the most powerful protection of the Mother of God the destiny of the human family, and, to this end, as you know ... We solemnly proclaimed the Assumption into heaven of the Virgin Mary, body and soul."

Pius XII continued to say that the "calamitous" times urge us to "fly with greater confidence to the Mother of God. There, the Christian people have always sought chief refuge in the hour of danger, because 'she has been constituted the cause of salvation for the whole human race' (St. Irenaeus)."

Pius XII looked to the coming month of October asking people

to raise their supplications to Mary by means of the Holy Rosary....

We well know the Rosary's powerful efficacy to obtain the maternal aid of the Virgin. By no means is there only one way to pray to obtain this aid. However, we consider the Holy Rosary the most convenient and most fruitful means, as is clearly suggested by the very origin of this practice, heavenly rather than human, and by its nature.

This pious pope also stressed the Rosary's major role in family life: "But above all it is in the bosom of the family that We desire the custom of the Holy Rosary to be everywhere adopted, religiously preserved, and ever more intensely practiced. In vain is a remedy sought for the wavering fate of civil life, if the family, the principle and foundation of the human community, is not fashioned after the pattern of the Gospel."

He concluded, "We do not hesitate to affirm again publicly that We put great confidence in the Holy Rosary for the healing of evils which afflict our times."

Isn't that a major teaching and counsel of Our Lady of Fatima?

Pius XII never relaxed in his Fatima devotion, trying to bring the message to everyone and trying to fulfill the requests. In 1952, as recorded in his July 7 apostolic letter *Sacro Vergente Anno*, he again consecrated Russia to the Most Blessed Virgin Mary. He did not, however, do it in union with the bishops of the world.

Pius XII increased and expanded "the cultus of the Mother of God in a way almost unparalleled in the history of the papacy,"[282] Father Hardon observed in 1952, with six years still to come in the Holy Father's reign.

On September 8, 1953, the feast of the Nativity of the Blessed Virgin Mary, Pius XII released his encyclical *Fulgens Corona*, which proclaimed a Marian year in celebration of the centenary of the definition of the dogma of the Immaculate Conception. Spanning 1954 to 1955, this was the first Marian Year ever declared for the Church.

---

[282] Hardon, "Pope Pius XII and Our Lady."

During the Marian Year, on October 11, the venerable pontiff honored Mary again with another title in his encyclical *Ad Caeli Reginam*, which proclaimed Mary's Queenship. He decreed and established her Queenship as a feast to be celebrated every May 31. (In 1969, it was moved to August 22, the octave of the Assumption.)

We can see a Fatima connection in the encyclical, as Pius XII wrote, "We likewise ordain that on the same day the consecration of the human race to the Immaculate Heart of the Blessed Virgin Mary be renewed, cherishing the hope that through such consecration a new era may begin, joyous in Christian peace and in the triumph of religion."[283]

Recall again that the consecration to the Immaculate Heart of Mary was a major Fatima request and, we might say, a directive.

Naturally, in that encyclical, Pius XII gave instructions. Among the directions for the faithful, he wrote, "May the beads of the Rosary be in the hands of all."[284] Is this not a major message and request of Our Lady of Fatima? Pius XII listened, and as the head of the Catholic Church, he promoted the Rosary.

Since nothing heaven does happens by chance, we can see providential affirmation of Pius XII as a Marian and Fatima pope. He died in October 1958, the month of the Holy Rosary. And he was buried in St. Peter's Basilica on October 13, the anniversary of the Miracle of the Sun.

Fulton Sheen's Revelation about Pius XII

One of the bishops at Fatima for the October 13, 1951, anniversary was Venerable Fulton Sheen. During a show on Fatima, as part of his popular *Life Is Worth Living* television series, he

[283] Pius XII, Encyclical *Ad Caeli Reginam* (October 11, 1954), no. 47.
[284] Ibid., no. 48.

described the impact of the October 13 apparition by saying, "The event itself might almost be called the birthday of the modern world because it was on that day the forces of good and evil seemed to reach their peak."

During the show, Bishop Sheen pointed out that he was wearing the pectoral cross worn by Bishop Eugenio Pacelli, the future Pope Pius XII, when he was nearly assassinated by Communists during his time as nuncio in Germany. Several men lay in wait for him in the house where he would arrive. Bishop Sheen described how once they saw their intended victim, the rattled assassin lost his gun, which Bishop Pacelli then fearlessly handed back to him. The would-be assassins fled. Pius XII would become a foe of Communism, which Our Lady so strongly warned of at Fatima, Sheen explained.

Participating in that 1951 Fatima anniversary with one million pilgrims praying all night in the rain, Bishop Sheen envisioned the hammer and sickle of Communism "changing its figure and symbolism and becoming, as the Book of the Apocalypse said, 'the moon under the Lady's feet.' This is the way to peace."[285]

Lucia and the Popes

Although Lucia had written down the Third Secret of Fatima in 1944, in obedience to her bishop and with permission of the Blessed Mother, she instructed that the letter could not be opened until 1960. In that year, Pope St. John XXIII, successor to Pius XII, opened and read it. But, as recounted in *Fatima for Today: The Urgent Marian Message of Hope*, by Fatima expert Father Andrew

---

[285] "Our Lady of Fatima—Ven. Bishop Fulton J. Sheen," excerpt from *Life Is Worth Living*, originally broadcast in 1954, video, 22:23, www.youtube.com/watch?v=YWzPU1oeViM.

Apostoli, the Holy Father decided not to reveal its contents. He did, however, institute the memorial of Our Lady of Fatima on May 13 on the liturgical calendar.

His successor Pope St. Paul VI also read the Third Secret, and he, too, decided against revealing it. On the golden jubilee of Fatima, May 13, 1967, Paul VI made a pilgrimage to the place of the apparitions, becoming the first pope to travel to Fatima. On that day, Paul VI greeted Sister Lucia and met briefly with her. He prayed with her, and she gave him a parchment, asking him to "intensify the prayer of the Rosary" and have it said in front of the Blessed Sacrament, as recounted in A *Pathway under the Gaze of Mary*.[286] Lucia never tired of following Our Lady's directives and promoting her messages from Fatima, as she was ever ready to follow the will of Jesus and Mary.

Also on that day, Pope Paul VI issued *Signum Magnum*, calling for everyone to renew their consecration to the Immaculate Heart of Mary. He noted that it was the twenty-fifth anniversary of the consecration of the Church and all mankind to the Immaculate Heart of Mary by Pius XII on October 31, 1942. Paul VI had renewed the consecration in 1964.

Now he asked everyone to renew their personal consecration, "to bring alive this most noble act of veneration through a life ever more consonant with the divine will and in a spirit of filial service and of devout imitation of their heavenly Queen."[287]

Then came Pope John Paul I. Lucia did not meet him during his reign as Holy Father, as it was so brief. She had met him, though, while he was still a cardinal when he visited the monastery where Lucia was cloistered. He and the others in the

---

[286] Carmel of Coimbra, A *Pathway*, 365.

[287] Paul VI, Apostolic Exhortation *Signum Magnum* (May 13, 1967).

delegation asked her to sign a holy card of the Heart of Mary for them.

Also, as Cardinal Joseph Ratzinger, Pope Benedict XVI visited and spoke with Sister Lucia in Coimbra in 1996. In 2008, just three years after her death, rather than the customary waiting period of five years, Benedict authorized the cause for Sister Lucia's beatification.

Two years later, during his homily on May 13, 2010, while saying Mass at Fatima, he told everyone, "We would be mistaken to think that Fatima's prophetic mission is complete."

On May 13, 2013, Pope Francis had his papacy dedicated to Our Lady of Fatima, and on October 13 of that year, he publicly had the world consecrated to the Blessed Virgin of Fatima.

The Fatima Pope

Of course, Pope St. John Paul II had a highly defined role in the promotion of the Fatima message. He, too, has been called "the Pope of Fatima" as much as "the Pope of Divine Mercy."

Sister Lucia met him in 1982 and again in 1991 at the Carmel in Fatima. She met with him yet again when he beatified Jacinta and Francisco on the feast of Our Lady of Fatima in 2000.

During their short conversation during the first visit, Lucia asked several things of John Paul II. Among them were the consecration of Russia and the beatification of her cousins. She gave him a few gifts, including rosaries that she had made and a picture of Our Lady.

During their second meeting, Sister Lucia had the unexpected opportunity to make one of those "duty" sacrifices. She did not like to have her picture taken, but there were a number of photographers ready to snap away when she and John Paul II were together. She went to remove herself, but the saintly Holy Father told her, "We have to oblige,"[288] and so she did so as a sacrificial offering. Then they went off to speak together privately.

The third visit took place when John Paul II beatified Jacinta and Francisco, and Cardinal Bertone and the bishop of Leiria-Fatima joined them. Lucia was given the letter of the Third Secret and asked to confirm that it was written by her. She confirmed that it was. Beforehand, she sent John Paul II another gift—three hundred rosaries that she had made.

It was a splendid occasion, bringing together those four saints in the making—a future pope-saint beatifying two children, soon to be canonized, and meeting with another potential saint, as Lucia's cause was opened not long after her death.

During his beatification homily, John Paul II again reminded us of some of Fatima's lessons. He explained how Francisco was motivated "to console Jesus and make him happy," using the young seer's words, since Jesus "is so sad because of the sins that are committed against him," and how Jacinta "had been so deeply moved by the vision of hell during the apparition of July 13 that no mortification or penance seemed too great to save sinners."

The sufferings that the three young children endured in the wake of the apparitions showed their trust in Our Lady. Even Lucia's mother treated her harshly for many months, thinking she was making up the apparitions. The children's perseverance was one of the lessons John Paul II shared.

"Ask your parents and teachers to enroll you in the 'school' of Our Lady, so that she can teach you to be like the little shepherds, who tried to do whatever she asked them," John Paul II advised the children attending the beatification. Quoting St. Louis de

---

[288] Ibid., 381.

Montfort, he added, "I tell you that 'one makes more progress in a short time of submission and dependence on Mary than during entire years of personal initiatives, relying on oneself alone.' This was how the little shepherds became saints so quickly."

Relying on Mary was key in John Paul's life, too—particularly on one fateful day in St. Peter's Square.

On the Fatima anniversary of May 13, 1981, John Paul II was shot by an assassin.

His first general audience after his recovery was held on October 7, when he reminded the faithful of the day's memorial of Our Lady of the Holy Rosary. He said he "became a debtor of the Blessed Virgin and all the patron saints," noting that the day of Fatima's anniversary was the day he was shot. He talked of the Rosary and how he "felt that extraordinary motherly protection and care, which turned out to be stronger than the deadly bullet." In addition, John Paul believed that he was the "bishop in white" that the Third Secret of Fatima mentioned.[289] He decided to release the Third Secret in 2000.

Years earlier on May 13, 1982, exactly a year after he was shot, John Paul II made a special trip to Fatima to thank Our Lady. In his stirring homily about Fatima during the anniversary Mass, he affirmed that there are no coincidences in the plans of Providence. He came to Fatima "especially in order to confess here the glory of God himself."

"If the Church has accepted the message of Fatima, it is, above all, because that message contains *a truth and a call* whose basic content is *the truth and the call of the Gospel itself*," John Paul II

---

[289] Part of the Third Secret of Fatima was the vision of a bishop dressed in white who was killed by soldiers. The children had the impression that the bishop was the pope.

stressed. "The message of Fatima is, in its basic nucleus, a call to *conversion and repentance*, as in the Gospel."

The Holy Father continued in that homily to reflect the Fatima message. He explained:

> The call to repentance is linked, as always, with a call to prayer. In harmony with the tradition of many centuries, the Lady of the message indicates the Rosary, which can rightly be defined as "Mary's prayer": the prayer in which she feels particularly united with us. She herself prays with us. The Rosary prayer embraces the problems of the Church, of the See of St. Peter, the problems of the whole world. In it, we also remember sinners, that they may be converted and saved, and the souls in purgatory.

John Paul II said that the call to repentance and conversion, "uttered in the Mother's message … is still more relevant than it was sixty-five years ago. It is still more urgent." Especially in today's times, it cries out to be heard and followed. "She calls us to accept her motherly help to return to the Source of redemption," he added.

It's very clear—Fatima is as relevant as ever—even more so.

Of course, John Paul II had nothing to do with Lucia's canonization cause because he outlived her by only about two months. She died on February 13, 2005, a Sunday. It was the same day of the month on which the Fatima apparitions took place. On that day, she had received a fax from John Paul II, sending words of comfort and his apostolic blessing. She held it and read it herself.

Just in time for the hundredth anniversary of Fatima on February 13, 2017, the diocesan phase of the canonization process for Sister Lucia officially closed. The date also marked the eleventh anniversary of Sister Lucia's death. The first part of her cause for canonization began in 2008, just three years after she died, thanks to the dispensation granted by Pope Benedict XVI.

It took from 2008 until 2017 to complete the necessary work because of the volumes of material that had to be examined. For one, there were the testimonies that had to be gathered from sixty witnesses concerning the holiness and heroic virtues of Sister Lucia. For another, all of her writings had to be gathered and examined.

"Each page that Sister Lucia wrote had to be meticulously analyzed, and we are talking of a universe of ten thousand letters that we managed to gather and of a diary with two thousand pages, in addition to other more personal texts," explained Sister Angela Coelho, the postulator for the cause of Sister Lucia's canonization. The process was bound to take a long time, as Lucia was, according to the vice-postulator of her cause, "a woman who lived almost 98 years, who corresponded with popes, since Pius XII to John Paul II, with cardinals," plus a great many others.[290]

That's quite a remarkable life for someone who was a shepherdess as a child. And it's quite a simple message she received and worked so tirelessly and valiantly to spread to the world, following the requests of Our Lord and Our Lady. Lucia wanted all of us to hear it. More than that, she wanted all of us, as Our Lady asked, to take it to heart and follow it. Our Lady told us what would happen if we did. It's all in the words of Fatima and in all the forgotten and providential connections from 1917 onward. Speaking of connections, there is another one—to Our Lady of Divine Mercy.

---

[290] Joseph Pronechen, "Sister Lucia of Fatima Takes Step toward Beatification," *National Catholic Register*, February 14, 2017, www. ncregister.com/blog/joseph-pronechen/sister-lucia-of-fatima-takes-step-toward-beatification.

13

Fatima and Divine Mercy

In 2017, the centennial of Our Lady's apparitions at Fatima brought to light a little realized but vital truth: Fatima and Divine Mercy are closely linked. Fewer than fifteen years after our Blessed Mother appeared at Fatima, and a mere two years after Mary and Jesus appeared to Sister Lucia in her convent in Spain, Our Lord began His revelations on Divine Mercy to St. Faustina.

Father Michael Gaitley of the Marians of the Immaculate Conception, the official promotors of the Divine Mercy devotion, points out one way the two devotions are related—by what we might call the "bookends" of Fatima. He said:

> In 1916, before the apparitions of Our Lady the next year, God sent the "Angel of Peace" to the three children of Fatima, telling them, "The Hearts of Jesus and Mary have *designs of mercy* on you." Thirteen years later, in what's often called "the last apparition of Fatima," Sister Lucia received a vision that included the words "grace and mercy."

"That the apparitions of Fatima would begin and end with mercy is fitting," Father Gaitley found. "After all, Our Lady of Fatima's merciful purpose was to prevent her children from having to go through terrible suffering."[291]

In his writings, Américo Pablo López-Ortiz, the international president of the World Apostolate of Fatima, similarly sees the integral harmony of Fatima and Divine Mercy. After all, the slogan of Fatima is "Grace and Mercy."[292]

The vital connection between Our Lady's message at Fatima and Our Lord's message of mercy becomes even clearer when we see other providential connections. López-Ortiz calls Pope St. John Paul II the protagonist of both devotions. As we recall, the pope was shot on May 13, 1981, an anniversary of Mary's first appearance at Fatima. He visited Fatima on the next anniversary to thank Our Lady for sparing his life through a miraculous intervention. He then championed the Fatima message and the Rosary.

On September 4, 1993, John Paul II visited the Shrine of the Gate of the Dawn (Ostrabrama) in Vilnius, Lithuania, and prayed the Rosary with other visitors before the miraculous icon of Our Lady of Mercy. There, in 1935, on the Sunday after Easter—now Divine Mercy Sunday—the image of Jesus, Divine Mercy, that St. Faustina had had painted according to His direction was shown and venerated publicly for the first time.

Both Son and Mother of Mercy were together in that one shrine—thus, eighteen years after Fatima, Jesus made the connection clear.

---

[291] Joseph Pronechen, "Fatima and Divine Mercy Are Eternally Linked," *National Catholic Register*, April 23, 2017, www.ncregister. com/daily-news/fatima-and-divine-mercy-are-eternally-linked.

[292] Américo Pablo López-Ortiz, "Fatima and Divine Mercy," www. worldfatima.com/images/FATIMA_AND_DIVINE_MERCY_-_ by_Prof._Americo.pdf.

The visionaries of Divine Mercy and Fatima themselves bear this connection out.

In her *Diary*, St. Faustina records a vision in which Mary said, "I am not only Queen of Heaven, but also the Mother of Mercy and your Mother" (330).

And at Fatima, as López-Ortiz revealed, the Fatima seers discovered "the infinite ocean of love and mercy that God is," and through Mary's heart, they discovered "the infinite mercy of God with poor sinners and the terrible threat they are facing, the existence of hell, created for those who proudly do not accept God's mercy."[293]

Mary told St. Faustina of the necessity of making God's mercy known: "You have to speak to the world about his great mercy.... Speak to souls about this great mercy while it is still the time for (granting) mercy" (*Diary* 635).

Jesus also told Faustina: "Before the Day of Justice I am sending the Day of Mercy.... I am prolonging the time of mercy for the sake of sinners. But woe to them if they do not recognize this time of my visitation" (*Diary* 1588, 1160). Faustina later understood that Jesus was prolonging the time of His mercy because of Mary's intercession.

Father Thomas McGlynn saw something similar when he was in Fatima. He believed that "the enormity of mankind's rebellion against God and God's infinite aversion for sin form the foundation of the Fatima message. Then He gives the sinner hope in the revelation that He will accept repentance made through the Immaculate Heart of Mary. Fatima manifests the most misunderstood of the divine attributes—justice and mercy." Our Lady "came to tell us how to keep out of hell!"[294]

---

[293] Ibid.

[294] McGlynn, *Vision of Fatima*, 203.

The Fruits of Fatima

The Divine Mercy devotion includes the Chaplet of Divine Mercy. This chaplet is prayed using rosary beads—a simple, tangible connection joining both devotions.

Father Gaitley also explained that the Chaplet should bear fruit in *deeds* of mercy. As Jesus told us through St. Faustina, "I demand from you deeds of mercy, which are to arise out of love for me" (*Diary* 742).

That can tie in to the sacrifices Fatima calls us to make. Thinking of the Holy Family vision in the October 13 apparition, we should recall how works of mercy can abound within the home: comforting a sick child or a spouse or being patient with those in error.

Recall the prayer that Our Lady taught the children to say after every decade of the Rosary: *O my Jesus, forgive us our sins, save us from the fires of hell; lead all souls to heaven, especially those who have most need of Your mercy.* Saying this prayer is a spiritual work of mercy and a direct connection to the message of Divine Mercy.

A final point—both devotions are prime calls to repentance.

"If there is one thing Our Lady stressed at Fatima, it was the imperative *repent*," wrote Father John Hardon. "That is what the sacrament of penance is all about."[295] It is one of the conditions of the Divine Mercy Sunday devotion, too.

We're also reminded of what John Paul II, "the Marian–Divine Mercy Pope," said when he visited Fatima in May 1982: "The evangelical call to repentance and conversion, uttered in the words of

---

[295] Fr. John A. Hardon, S.J., "Living the Fatima Message," excerpted from a presentation at the 1991 National Fatima Symposium, Felician College, Lodi, NJ, posted at The Real Presence Association, http://www.therealpresence.org/archives/Mariology/Mariology_042.htm.

the Mother, is always present." So is Jesus' message of Divine Mercy. Where the Son is, the Mother is. Where the Mother is, the Son is.

Heaven gave us one more confirmation through John Paul II when he died on April 2, 2005. That day was the first Saturday of the month and at the hour, the end of the Vigil Mass of Divine Mercy Sunday. Heaven was going to welcome the pope who promoted the Rosary and who wore the brown scapular — the pope of Fatima and of Divine Mercy.

14

Fatima Conquers Foes

At Fatima, the words "spiritual battle" were not used, though they were implied; we are part of one such battle, whether we admit it or not, and Our Lady gave us all the directions we need to be victorious. Recall that she identified herself on October 13 in the final apparition as Our Lady of the Rosary. That title grew out of the Battle of Lepanto in 1571, which was fought to save Christianity in Europe. Pope St. Pius V asked for a Holy League to form and meet the threat, and he asked Catholics to pray the Rosary. The Catholic fleet all prayed the Rosary, asking for Our Lady's intercession. Pius V and all the leaders attributed that David-versus-Goliath victory, saving Christianity and Western civilization, to Our Lady. To commemorate this historic battle, he instituted the feast of Our Lady of Victories, soon renamed Our Lady of the Rosary.

At Fatima, Our Lady of the Rosary came to save us again, and she gave us the weapons for victory. St. Padre Pio called the Rosary "the Weapon." Pius XI — remember how at Fatima Our Lady mentioned an upcoming pope to be named Pius XI? — reminded us that holy people have used the Rosary "as a powerful weapon to put the demons to flight, to preserve the integrity of life, to acquire virtue more easily, and in a word to attain real peace among men." He added that he always gave rosaries to the newly married, recommending the prayer to them and encouraging them, "citing Our own example, not to let even one day pass without saying the Rosary, no matter how burdened they may be with many cares and labors."[296]

Bishop Fulton Sheen revealed, "The power of the Rosary is beyond description."[297]

But, as in past battles, the apparitions of Fatima did not go without some adversity, especially in the form of opposition and attacks by atheists and Freemasons. It was to be expected, because there was a spiritual battle being carried out.

Even after the Miracle of the Sun on October 13, the enemies of religion and anti-clerics, who were vocal and in positions of power in Portugal at the time, didn't let up on their attacks. In *The True Story of Fatima*, Father John de Marchi describes how these men, at their Masonic lodge in a town near Fatima, planned to mock what had been happening at the Cova da Iria.

But Fatima's enemies got the tables turned on them. A major Lisbon paper, *Diario de Noticias*, reported what they did on the night of October 23, 1917, at the Cova da Iria. They cut down the tree that they identified as the one where the children experienced the apparitions of Our Lady. They carted it away along with a wooden arch, the lanterns around it, and some other religious articles left in the area. Then they displayed them to discredit the children and the apparitions.

---

[296] Pius XI, Encyclical *Ingravescentibus Malis* (September 29, 1937), nos. 14, 29.
[297] Bishop Fulton Sheen, *The World's First Love* (New York: McGraw-Hill, 1952), 189.

They got a big surprise, however, when even the critics of the Church saw their actions as disgraceful. But the biggest surprise for them? In her memoirs, Lucia revealed that the men got orders

> to pull down these poles [on which people hung lanterns to watch over the site] and also cut down the holm oak on which the apparitions had taken place and drag it away with them behind a car. In the morning, news of what had happened spread like wildfire. I ran to the place to see if it were true. But what was my delight to find that the poor men had made a mistake, and that instead of cutting down the holm oak, they had carried off one of the others growing nearby![298]

Lucia then did something else quite surprising: "I then asked Our Lady to forgive these poor men, and I prayed for their conversion."[299]

That was not the only attempt to interfere with the apparitions and the message of Fatima. We already saw how the August apparition was delayed because the children were kidnapped, taken to prison, and threatened with torture and death if they did not reveal the secrets the Blessed Mother had entrusted to them. And we saw how that ended. The atheists and secularists got nowhere.

Then, a few years after the apparitions, disbelieving monsters struck again, this time at the Little Chapel of Apparitions at the Cova da Iria. Father Agostino Marques Ferreira, a priest there, described in two letters on March 6 and 8, 1922, what took place: "It was before daybreak when the explosion of the bomb

---

[298] *Memoirs*, 106.
[299] Ibid.

was heard," he wrote on that first date.[300] Railings around the altar were yanked out, as were the railings protecting the holm oak tree. The chapel caught fire.

In his second letter, the priest said he had found an explosive device, possibly a grenade, that "the scoundrels left in the enclosure where the stump of the holm oak is."

He believed that four bombs were put into the chapel's side walls to destroy it. But the walls only cracked and remained standing. The pulpit, too, remained intact.

Father Ferreira minced no words: "Since the atrocity committed at the little chapel of Our Lady is above all an affront to the Most Holy Virgin and to the faith of the people, you, Reverend Father, will, on the coming Sunday, invite the faithful to make reparation to our heavenly Mother, going there on the thirteenth in a true pilgrimage of penance. On that day, let there be sung the Litany of All the Saints and the Merciful Lord God!"[301]

There happened a certain phenomenon thought miraculous on that March 6 in connection with this explosion. It was similar to another phenomenon that occurred in connection with an attack less than four months earlier in Mexico at the Shrine of Our Lady of Guadalupe. There, on November 14, 1921, a man placed what looked like a bouquet of flowers in front of the miraculous image of Our Lady of Guadalupe. It was actually a bomb. It exploded and damaged the marble altar steps, the brass candlesticks, and the heavy crucifix. The crucifix took the impact of the explosion and fell to the ground. Behind it, the image of Our Lady of Guadalupe remained safe. Not only was it

---

[300] Martins, *Documents on Fatima*, 259.
[301] Ibid.

undamaged, but even the glass in front of it was not shattered. It was Jesus protecting His Mother.

What else happened at Fatima in the Cova that day in March? The statue of Our Lady of Fatima, the very first one, was also miraculously undamaged — not a scratch. Heaven had the last laugh. Jesus protected His Mother once again. And how did He do it this time?

That evening, for some reason, the person who guarded the statue had an inspiration to take the statue of Our Lady to a safe spot, so he took it home. The statue was not even in the chapel during the time of the explosion!

Not only did the attempt to destroy the devotion of the people fail, but the opposite happened — people only became even more devoted.

In fact, this statue of Our Lady of Fatima in the Chapel of Apparitions, which has been venerated since June 13, 1920, was solemnly crowned on May 13, 1946, and, later, St. John Paul II placed in the crown the bullet that was meant to assassinate him on May 13, 1981, and he thanked Our Lady for saving his life.

Obviously, Our Lady was victorious over all the Fatima attacks. Her Fatima message is one of victory — a loving message she would bring to all the world, even by way of her visits through her International Pilgrim Virgin Statue. In fact, a Fatima pope had something to say about this.

The background: Portugal's premiere sculptor, Jóse Thedim, carved that first statue of Our Lady in 1920. Then, for the 1946 crowning by Pope Pius XII's representative, Lucia let it be known that Our Lady had a brighter, shining edge on her mantle. With that, Bishop da Silva had her speak with Thedim to carve a new statue according to her description. It included a star at the tunic's hem. This new image became the International Pilgrim

Virgin Statue that began traveling to people who could not get to Fatima, Portugal. And Thedim carved two more, which were blessed by the bishop of Fatima.

Then, on October 13, 1951, speaking over the radio to the people in Fatima, Pius XII said, "In 1946, I crowned Our Lady at Fatima as Queen of the World, and the following year through the Pilgrim Virgin, she set forth as though to claim Her dominion, and the favors she performs along the way are such that We can hardly believe what We are seeing with Our eyes."[302]

---

[302] World Apostolate of Fatima, "History of the International Pilgrim Virgin Statue," www.fatimatourforpeace.com/wp-content/uploads/2016/02/History-of-the-Statue.pdf; and www.fatimatourforpeace.com/the-statue/.

15

Consecration of Russia — Yes or No?

Any look at Fatima would also need at least a short mention of the consecration of Russia. In 1917, the three Fatima children lived in the countryside, in a small village. They were busy with tending sheep and doing their chores. They were very young at the time, which makes it quite easy to understand that when Our Lady told them about the consecration of Russia, they didn't know what that referred to. We get a glimpse of what their initial reaction was when, years later, Lucia was in the Carmel in Coimbra.

Dr. Branca Paul, Sister Lucia's personal physician for the last fifteen years of the nun's life, saw her patient daily. Lucia often talked to Dr. Paul about her days as a young child, usually spent with her cousins Jacinta and Francisco. One time, when speaking with Dr. Paul about the apparitions, Lucia began laughing.

"In speaking about Our Lady's warnings about the 'errors of Russia,'" Dr. Paul said, "Lucia would tell me that she and Jacinta thought 'Russia' was an evil woman."[303] Not only does this revelation cause a chuckle, but the fact that the children in the

---

[303] "Sister Lucia: 'Mary's Witness,'" The Divine Mercy, www.the-divinemercy.org/news/Sister-Lucia-Marys-Witness-2937.

peasant village had no idea of who or what Russia was becomes another proof that the apparitions were genuine.

Concerning the consecration of Russia, in *A Pathway under the Gaze of Mary*, we learn that Lucia wrote to her confessor in 1936, telling him that she asked the Lord why He did not convert Russia Himself without the Holy Father making the consecration.

As we've seen earlier, Our Lord answered, "Because I want my whole Church to acknowledge this consecration as a triumph of the Immaculate Heart of Mary, in order to later extend its cult and to place devotion to this Immaculate Heart alongside devotion to my Sacred Heart."[304]

During the July 13, 1917, apparition, Our Lady, for the first time, gave the preventative measure to employ against errors when she said:

> To prevent this, I shall come to the world to ask that Russia be consecrated to my Immaculate Heart, and I shall ask that on the first Saturday of every month Communions of reparation be made in atonement for the sins of the world. If my wishes are fulfilled, Russia will be converted, and there will be peace; if not, then Russia will spread her errors throughout the world, bringing new wars and persecution of the Church; the good will be martyred, and the Holy Father will have much to suffer; certain nations will be annihilated. But in the end my Immaculate Heart will triumph. The Holy Father will consecrate Russia to me, and she will be converted, and the world will enjoy a period of peace.

[304] Carmel of Coimbra, *A Pathway*, 187.

What did Lucia do after she was able to make this message known? She explained how the bishop of Leiria and her superior ordered her to write her first letter to Pius XII, requesting the consecration of Russia to the Immaculate Heart of Mary. She did that in 1940, telling the Holy Father that Our Lord requested that the pope "consecrate the world to the Immaculate Heart of Mary, with a special mention for Russia, and order that all the bishops of the world do the same in union with Your Holiness."[305]

On October 31, 1942, Pope Pius XII made a consecration of the world to the Immaculate Heart of Mary. The bishops of Portugal, assembled in Lisbon's cathedral, joined him.

The Holy Father did make the consecration to the Immaculate Heart of Mary; it was not done in union with all the bishops in the world, however. He consecrated all peoples, and, although he did not use the specific word "Russia," his words and descriptions in one section unmistakably signified that country.

Still, it made a difference in the world, as Sister Lucia would reveal, saying that the Lord was delighted, and even though the act was not completed fully, as requested, He would "bring an end soon to the war." In fact, very quickly after the consecration, the tide of World War II began to turn in favor of the Allies.

Ten years later, on July 7, 1952, Pius XII again explicitly consecrated the Russian people to the Immaculate Heart of Mary in his Apostolic Letter *Sacro Vergente Anno*. But this time, too, he did not do it in union with the bishops of the world.

Eventually, the consecration was made at St. Peter's Basilica by John Paul II on March 25, 1984. Sister Lucia wrote clearly that

[305] Martins, *Documents of Fatima*, 378, 386.

this consecration was accepted by heaven. But though the answer was given that heaven accepted the consecration as done by John Paul II, there remains controversy about this. We won't delve into the controversy here, but I think it is safe to believe what Lucia herself believed regarding John Paul II's act of consecration.

16

Our Lady of Akita and Today's Crisis—A Fatima Reminder

Fifty-six years later, nearly 6,700 miles to the East, there was an echo that began in Portugal.

On October 13, 1973, the anniversary of Our Lady's last apparition at Fatima and the Miracle of the Sun, she appeared to Sister Agnes Sasagawa in a convent in Akita, Japan. It was a Saturday—Our Lady's special day of the week. Our Lady's warning during this apparition was most dire. First, though, let's take a quick look at what happened to Sister Agnes in 1969 when she was in a hospital. As she was praying a Rosary, her guardian angel surprised her and taught her to prayer after each decade, "O my Jesus, forgive us our sins; save us from the fires of hell; and lead all souls to heaven, especially those most in need."[306]

Right away there are echoes of Fatima. Not only because of the manifestation of her guardian angel to teach her this prayer that the Blessed Mother taught the Fatima children, but for an additional unusual reason, because at that point, the nun could not have been familiar with Fatima. When a priest heard her

[306] John Haffert, *The Meaning of Akita* (Asbury, NJ: 101 Foundation, 1989), 2–3.

praying this prayer after each decade, he knew it was the prayer taught at Fatima. What's more, he "was amazed that Agnes knew it because it had not yet been published in Japan."[307]

As Sister Agnes knelt in the chapel to pray the Rosary, Our Lady said to her:

> The work of the devil will infiltrate even into the Church in such a way that one will see cardinals opposing cardinals, bishops against bishops. The priests who venerate me will be scorned and opposed by their confreres ... churches and altars sacked; the Church will be full of those who accept compromises, and the demon will press many priests and consecrated souls to leave the service of the Lord.[308]
>
> The demon will be especially implacable against souls consecrated to God. The thought of the loss of so many souls is the cause of my sorrow. If sins increase in number and gravity, there will be no longer pardon for them.

We will look at this last sentence in a moment.

Our Lady also told Sister Agnes:

> As I told you, if men do not repent and better themselves, the Father will inflict a terrible punishment on all humanity. It will be a punishment greater than the deluge, such as one will never have seen before. Fire will fall from the sky and will wipe out a great part of humanity, the good as well as the bad, sparing neither priests nor faithful. The survivors will find themselves so desolate that they will

---

[307] Ibid., 2.

[308] Fr. Teiji Yasuda, O.S.V., and John M. Haffert, *Akita: The Tears and Message of Mary* (Asbury, NJ: 101 Foundation, 1989), 78.

envy the dead. The only arms which will remain for you will be the Rosary and the Sign left by my Son. Each day recite the prayers of the Rosary. With the Rosary, pray for the Pope, the bishops, and priests.

A terrible, dreadful warning it is! Reflecting on the Miracle of the Sun, Father Regis Scanlon said, "No doubt, the rain and the sun at Fatima symbolized the flood at the time of Noah and the fire at the time of Lot. The message of Fatima is: if people do not change their ways, God will once again have to purify the world leaving only a remnant that is good."[309]

At Fatima, too, in her July apparition, Our Lady warned of the possibility that "various nations will be annihilated." Our Mother told us, her children, the equivalent of "don't play with fire." But did we listen? We suffered World War II, which she predicted during her July apparition, and which ended in Japan with the unthinkable: a nuclear explosion. She reminded us again with strong words at Akita. Have we listened?

During the thirty-fifth anniversary year of Fatima, Bishop Fulton Sheen gave us several insights into ways the Miracle of the Sun fits into this picture, first reminding us that Jesus sent Our Lady of Fatima, "his Mother, to save us."[310] Although his words came just over two decades before Akita, because of the Fatima connection they seem proper to both.

Looking at three possible interpretations of the Miracle of the Sun, Sheen said that the first possibility is "to regard it as

---

[309] Fr. Regis Scanlon, O.F.M.Cap., "Fatima and the 'Signs of the Times' Needs a Closer Look," Homiletic and Pastoral Review, January 30, 2017, www.hprweb.com/2017/01/fatima-and-the-signs-of-the-times-needs-a-closer-look/.

[310] Sheen, *The World's First Love*, 242.

a warning of the atomic bomb, which like a falling sun, would darken the world."

In contrast, the miracle "could be seen as a sign of hope, namely, that the Woman who came out of nature is mightier than the forces of nature. The atomic bomb explodes through fission ... but atomic fission is the way the sun lights the world.... At Fatima, the fact that Mary could take this great seat and center of atomic power and make it her plaything, the fact that she could swing the sun 'like a trinket at her wrist,' is a proof that God has given her power over it, not for death, but for light and life and hope. As Scripture foretold, 'And now, in heaven, a great portent appeared: a woman that wore the sun for her mantle (Rev. 12:1)."[311]

The third possibility is again, more dire: "to regard it as a miniature and a cameo of what may yet happen to the world, namely, some sudden cataclysm or catastrophe which would make the world shake in horror as the 70,000 shook at Fatima that day. On Oct 13, 1917, believers and unbelievers prostrated themselves upon the ground during the Miracle of the Sun, most of them pleasing to God for Mercy and Forgiveness. That whirlwind sun ... may have been the harbinger of a world spectacle that will draw millions to their knees in a rebirth of faith."[312]

Naturally, we don't want choice one or choice three to happen. The vital and essential response has been told and handed to us over and over.

At Fatima, Our Lady had already spelled out what we need to do to avert these kinds of conflicts, and she repeated the same ideas during this visit to Akita on Oct. 13, 1973. The Rosary

[311] Ibid., 243.
[312] Ibid., 243–245.

is the way. So is reparation. They are the rock foundation to build upon.

At Akita, Our Lady concluded with these words, offering hope and a promise too: "Pray very much the prayers of the Rosary. I alone am able still to save you from the calamities which approach. Those who place their confidence in me will be saved."[313]

Connecting the Dots — Warnings and the Solution

At Fatima, on July 13, Our Lady prophesied that if men did not refrain from offending God, another and more terrible war would begin during the pontificate of Pius XI.

In her messages, our Blessed Mother calls us to conversion, much as John the Baptist did. And Jesus' first declaration in His public ministry is "Repent and believe in the good news." Because many people did not listen to Our Lady's advice or put it into practice, her prophetic warning came true with World War II.

Our Lady began that July apparition by saying, "Continue to say the Rosary every day in honor of Our Lady of the Rosary, to obtain the peace of the world and the end of the war, because only she can obtain it."

Remember how she said it at Akita? "I alone am able still to save you from the calamities which approach."[314]

Today's religious, cultural, and political wars — especially those against God's laws and commandments — show that we still are not listening in sufficient numbers to our Mother.

In her three apparitions at Akita, Our Lady warned us more than once. On August 3, she said, "Many men in this world afflict the Lord. I desire souls to console Him to soften the anger of the

---

[313] Yasuda, *Akita*, 78.
[314] Ibid.

The Fruits of Fatima

Heavenly Father. I wish, with my Son, for souls who will repair by their suffering and their poverty for the sinners and ingrates."[315] Remember that Our Lady called for reparation at Fatima, too.

Continuing the Akita message, she said:

> In order that the world might know His anger, the Heavenly Father is preparing to inflict a great chastisement on all mankind. With my Son I have intervened so many times to appease the wrath of the Father. I have prevented the coming of calamities by offering Him the sufferings of the Son on the Cross, His Precious Blood, and beloved souls who console Him, forming a cohort of victim souls. Prayer, penance, and courageous sacrifices can soften the Father's anger.[316]

Our Lady also said, "Pray very much for the pope, bishops, and priests. Since your Baptism you have always prayed faithfully for them. Continue to pray very much … very much."[317]

Bishop John Shojiro Ito formally approved the Akita apparitions. As he told a group of pilgrims and he repeated to a questioner, "It is the message of Fatima."[318]

To make this connection even clearer, let's look at events associated with the Akita apparitions.

On June 12, while in the chapel, Sister Agnes saw brilliant light coming from the tabernacle. The same happened on the following two days. Take note of the name of her congregation: the Handmaids of the Eucharist.

---

[315] Ibid., 145.
[316] Ibid., 62, 195.
[317] Ibid., 36.
[318] Ibid., 199; Haffert, *The Meaning of Akita*, 1.

Then, on July 6, again while praying in the chapel, Sister Agnes heard a voice coming from the statue of the Blessed Virgin Mary. The same day, some other Sisters saw drops of blood coming from the statue's right hand. This phenomenon occurred four times. The wound in the statue's hand remained visible until it disappeared on September 29.

At the same time, the statue also started to "sweat." Then, sixteen months and a few days after Our Lady's October 13 message, on January 4, 1975 — again a Saturday — the statue of the Blessed Mother started to weep and went on to do so 101 times, until the tears stopped on September 15, 1981. Remember, September 15 is the feast of Our Lady of Sorrows. Our Lady appeared as Our Lady of Sorrows on October 13, 1917, at Fatima.

Now for that promised look at the "no longer pardon" part of the Akita message. John Haffert explained it in relation to the sin against the Holy Spirit. He said, quoting John Paul II's encyclical on the Holy Spirit, "It is because this non-forgiveness is linked, as to its cause, to non-repentance, in other words to the radical refusal to be converted." John Paul II explains that sins against the Holy Spirit are those "committed by the person who claims to have a right to persist in evil, in any sin at all, and who thus rejects Redemption."

Haffert reminds us that people today are "claiming the right to sin." He lists areas including abortion, artificial contraception, and "denying God's teachings to children." This was in the early 1990s. The world has added tremendously to the list since then.

Hope Abounds

Haffert also explains how God sent his Mother, as Mother of Mercy, a sign of hope that all is not lost. What happens now depends on how we respond. She can intercede to avoid or soften such a dire chastisement as she described at Akita: "I alone am able still to save you from the calamities which approach. Those who place their confidence in me will be saved."

She told us at Fatima, too, that she will win in the end—her Immaculate Heart will triumph. Our Lady came to Fatima and later to Akita because she wants us to join her in victory.

It's as if St. Bernard knew centuries earlier what was going to happen when Fatima arrived, because he would teach everyone, "When you follow Mary, there is no straying from the way; when you pray to her, there is no cause to despair; if she holds your hand, you will not fall; and if she protects you, there is no need to fear."[319]

Considering what Our Lady asks us to do, Haffert rightly said that her messages "were addressed especially to Catholics. From them, above all, there must be a response. If they refuse, do they not deserve the chastisement along with the 'bad'?" But if we listen and follow Our Lady's instructions, that still can be prevented. Or at least the suffering can be lessened.

Writing about the latter times, the great Marian St. Louis de Montfort explained:

> Mary must shine forth more than ever in mercy, power, and grace; in mercy, to bring back and welcome lovingly the poor sinners and wanderers who are to be converted and return to the Catholic Church; in power, to combat the enemies of God who will rise up menacingly to seduce and crush by promises and threats all those who oppose them; finally, she must shine forth in grace to inspire and

---

[319] Father Hardon, "Our Lady of Fatima in the Light of History."

support the valiant soldiers and loyal servants of Jesus Christ who are fighting for His cause.

What Our Lady said at Fatima during her July apparition goes for Akita too: "If you do what I tell you, many souls will be saved, and there will be peace."

Simple Solution, Simple Request

Akita is a strong reminder of Fatima. It happened in a slightly different way, but Akita's solution is Fatima's solution. Fatima's instructions are Akita's instructions. They are really very simple.

Fatima and Akita give us the simple instructions we need to follow: "Pray very much the prayers of the Rosary," Our Lady instructed at Akita. And again, "Each day recite the prayers of the Rosary. With the Rosary, pray for the pope, the bishops, and priests."

Our Lady requested the Rosary at each of her apparitions in Fatima. For one, she said, "Continue to say the Rosary every day in honor of Our Lady of the Rosary to obtain the peace of the world and the end of the war, because only she can obtain it."

Also, she requested that we be consecrated to her Immaculate Heart and to be enrolled in and to wear the brown scapular, showing our dedication to Our Lady.

Further, we must make sacrifices in reparation for sin. Remember the counsel and instruction connected with Fatima? We were told that the sacrifices required are those of fulfilling our daily duties. So we should begin the day with the traditional Morning Offering, which includes everything you do.

We ought to have a devotion to St. Joseph. And we should make the Five First Saturdays devotion, fulfilling its simple conditions.

The Fruits of Fatima

If enough people respond to Mary's message, the triumph of her Immaculate Heart will be sooner rather than later. In her second appearance at Fatima, she assured us, "I will be with you always, and my Immaculate Heart will be your comfort and the way which will lead you to God." Then she guaranteed, "In the end my Immaculate Heart will triumph."

17

Know, Act, Hope

We've looked at many forgotten or little-known facts of Fatima that, in some way or another, relate the message, strengthen the message, or inspire us to take the message to heart and practice the requests and life-giving directives of Our Lady. We all have a decision to make. First, let's step back and recap a few high points during the apparitions of Our Lady that can steer us in the right direction.

Let's start by recalling a lesson embedded in details that are easily dismissed because they seem so unimportant, so mundane, such as the fact that the children were shepherds. Yet who were the first to learn about the birth of Jesus in Bethlehem? That's right, the shepherds tending their flocks. The angel announced His birth to them, and they "went in haste and found Mary and Joseph, and the infant lying in the manger" (Luke 2:16). That connects with the October apparition, when the Holy Family appeared together. If the shepherds went "in haste," we should also hasten to live the messages that the Good Shepherd's Mother, Mary, brought to us at Fatima. She came to the shepherds with her message, not just for the three children but for the whole world, so that we all may become "the sheep of His pasture." Our Lady wants the many lost sheep to be found so that the Good

Shepherd can call his friends and say, "Rejoice with me because I have found my lost sheep" (Luke 15:6).

When Our Lord was born, the shepherds didn't keep the message to themselves. Luke adds "All who heard it were amazed by what had been told them by the shepherds" (2:18). We should tell others about Our Lady's message, as the three shepherd children of Fatima did.

At the same time, why might Our Lady have chosen to appear to children again, as she had in other approved apparitions? Maybe it was to remind us of what Jesus told the apostles: "Whoever does not accept the kingdom of God like a child will not enter it" (Luke 18:17). Lucia, Jacinta, and Francisco certainly accepted the words and directions of Our Lady concerning the Kingdom of God right from the first apparition.

We have to develop that childlike trust and believe Our Lady of Fatima, our Blessed Mother, and her requests—and not just believe, but act on them, as the Fatima children did. Like them, we need to accept and respond to the messages as the kind of trusting children that her Son, Our Lord, clearly instructed us to be.

Father Frederick Miller explains it this way: "The teaching of Mary at Fatima was perfectly adapted to the capacity of the children yet able to be of benefit to every member of the Church, including the most intellectual and sophisticated." He adds, "The scriptural doctrine of the 'two ways' is at the heart of the Fatima message. Each person must make a choice: the way to life or the way to death; unbelief and rebellion or faith and conversion; self or Christ; hell or heaven."[320]

---

[320] Miller, "Mary: Catechist at Fatima."

During a radio interview, Servant of God Father John Hardon found the answer to why many weren't attentive to the Fatima message and requests of Our Lady near the end of the twentieth century. He lamented that "modern man has reached a point in history that I do not hesitate to call self-idolatry.... Even once-Christian countries are becoming rapidly paganized.... The modern world is practicing the most insidious form of idolatry, the worship of self."[321]

This choice Father Miller presents goes all the way back to the beginnings of Scripture. After leading the people for forty years through the desert, before they entered the Promised Land, Moses addressed them in clear terms. He explained to them the two ways they could follow, warned them against idolatry, and mapped out which spiritual road would lead them to the Promised Land of Heaven. He told them if they obeyed the Lord and His commandments he would have compassion on them, shower blessings upon them, and restore their fortunes.

"See," Moses echoed, "I have set before you life and death, the blessing and the curse. Choose life, then, that you and your descendants may live" (Deut. 30:15, 19).

Naturally, Our Lady of Fatima came to show us to choose life.

One more point before moving on. During his interview, Father Hardon said that he believed "Fatima is especially the sign in our age of the moral miracles that God wants to work in a proud, self-preoccupied, pleasure-intoxicated mankind." And how? Our Lady wants her Son Jesus to work tremendous moral miracles. "Mary is capable of working such miracles."

Now for that promised recap.

---

[321] Father Hardon, "An Interview: Jesuit Theologian and Author."

The Fruits of Fatima

May 13: "Please don't be afraid of me, I'm not going to harm you," were Our Lady's first words to Lucia, Jacinta, and Francisco when she appeared for the first time on May 13.

Mary's words perfectly echo what we find in the Bible, from the Old to the New Testament. Among the many examples are these: God says to Israel, "Do not fear: I am with you" (Isa. 41:10); Jesus tells the synagogue official, "Do not be afraid; just have faith" (Mark 5:36); Jesus calms His apostles on the sea, saying, "Take courage, it is I, do not be afraid!" (Mark 6:50); and Jesus bolsters their faith at the Last Supper with this reminder: "Do not let your hearts be troubled or afraid" (John 14:27). Mary hears from the angel Gabriel, "Do not be afraid, Mary, for you have found favor with God" (Luke 1:30).

"Please don't be afraid of me, I'm not going to harm you," Mary assures the children—as she assures us. She came for our good, for our salvation.

"Say the Rosary every day, to bring peace to the world and an end to the war," Mary told the children.

Our Lady appeared at the Cova da Iria. Father Martins noted that "Cova da Iria" derives from the Greek word *eirene*, meaning "peace." "Thus it can be affirmed in a way," he says, "that Our Lady appeared, during the First World War, in the Cove of Peace."[322] And she meant for that peace not just to bring an end to World War I but to extend continuously throughout the world, beginning in our hearts, in our families, and in our towns, cities, and countries, if we follow her directions.

June 13: "I want you to continue saying the Rosary every day," was the directive Mary gave to the three children when she appeared a month later, on June 13.

---

[322] Martin, *Documents of Fatima*, 133.

Then our Blessed Mother taught them to add this prayer to the Rosary, telling them, "And after each one of the mysteries, my children, I want you to pray in this way: 'O my Jesus, forgive us our sins, save us from the fires of hell; lead all souls to heaven, especially those who have most need of Your mercy.'" Our Blessed Mother was asking all of us to follow these instructions.

She also said, "Jesus wishes you to make me known and loved on earth. He wishes also for you to establish devotion in the world to my Immaculate Heart." We learn from her that devotion to the Immaculate Heart of Mary is necessary and very pleasing to God.

July 13: "Make sacrifices for sinners, and say often, especially while making a sacrifice: 'O Jesus, this is for love of Thee, for the conversion of sinners, and in reparation for offenses committed against the Immaculate Heart of Mary.'"

So instructed Our Lady. Mary said much during this July visit, largely concentrating on helping sinners and encouraging devotion to her Immaculate Heart. She made the lesson very striking, showing graphically where sinners end up: "You have seen hell, where the souls of poor sinners go. It is to save them that God wants to establish in the world devotion to my Immaculate Heart. If you do what I tell you, many souls will be saved, and there will be peace."

Mary made this plain to the children and to us. There was no holding back, even from young children, the dreadful possibly of losing heaven. But she also revealed the way to gain it and to help others to get back on the right path: "Continue to say the Rosary every day in honor of Our Lady of the Rosary to obtain the peace of the world and the end of the war, because only she can obtain it."

During this visit, Our Lady also made known this must-do request: "I shall ask that on the first Saturday of every month

The Fruits of Fatima

Communions of reparation be made in atonement for the sins of the world."

She also made another reference to her Immaculate Heart, this time connected with the consecration of Russia. If her wishes were fulfilled, there would be conversion and peace. If not, the world would experience the spread of errors, wars, persecution of the Church, and martyrdom; the Holy Father would suffer much; and nations would be annihilated.

We've got to understand how important devotion to the Immaculate Heart of Mary is. She tells us herself. She tells us that God wants us to have that devotion. How much clearer can it be?

August 19: "Continue to say the Rosary every day," Our Lady again reminded us during her August visit, delayed because the children were taken to jail the morning of August 13 when the visit should have taken place. She also spoke about celebrating the feast of Our Lady of the Rosary.

"Pray, pray very much. Make sacrifices for sinners. Many souls go to hell, because no one is willing to help them with sacrifice," our Blessed Mother continued to teach us. Very clearly, over and over, our Mother bids us to pray the Rosary, to pray and sacrifice for sinners, to honor her Immaculate Heart, and to make the First Saturday devotions.

September 13: "Continue the Rosary, my children. Say it every day that the war may end," our Blessed Mother again told us.

Then she added that the following month she would appear also as Our Lady of Sorrows and Our Lady of Mount Carmel. Mary was certainly telling us of the importance of her brown scapular by appearing as Our Lady of Mount Carmel.

"Our Lord will come, as well as Our Lady of Dolors and Our Lady of Carmel. St. Joseph will appear with the Child Jesus to bless the world," she also said. She would be standing by them—a beautiful reference to the Holy Family and the importance of family.

October 13: Lucia asked what Our Lady requested, and Our Lady first answered, "I want a chapel built here in my honor." Then Our Lady followed with her constant monthly instruction: "I want you to continue saying the Rosary every day." How can we not believe in the importance of this directive if our Blessed Mother Mary repeats it to us so frequently? Doesn't it show us her motherly concern for us in the way she teaches and guides us?

Next, she told the children, "The war [World War I] will end soon, and the soldiers will return to their homes." Then she identified herself as she had promised, saying, "I am the Lady of the Rosary."

Then Our Lady of the Rosary reminds us once again, "People must amend their lives and ask pardon for their sins. They must not offend our Lord anymore, for He is already too much offended!" Remember, in July, Our Lady told the children "if men do not refrain from offending God," there would be another and more terrible war (World War II).

These important requests are the bidding of Our Lady of Fatima, Our Lady of the Rosary, the most loving of mothers, directing us toward what is ultimately our own good—repent, don't offend Our Lord anymore, pray the Rosary daily, have devotion to her Immaculate Heart, pray and sacrifice for sinners, do the Five First Saturdays devotion. It's clear and simple. Anybody can do this. We've gone over all the forgotten details and the explanations of why and how.

St. John Paul II said during his homily at Fatima on May 13, 1982, "Mary's appeal is not for just once.... It must be unceasingly returned to. It must ever be taken up anew."

Now it's up to all of us to start afresh, to start anew, to follow Our Lady of Fatima.

Appendix

Fatima Prayers

Decade Prayer

O my Jesus, forgive us our sins, save us from the fires of hell; lead all souls to heaven, especially those who have most need of Your mercy.

Pardon Prayer

My God, I believe, I adore, I hope, and I love Thee! I beg pardon for all those who do not believe, do not adore, do not hope and do not love Thee.

Angel's Prayer

Most Holy Trinity, Father, Son, and Holy Spirit, I adore You profoundly, and I offer You the most precious Body, Blood, Soul, and Divinity of Jesus Christ, present in all the tabernacles of the world, in reparation for the outrages, sacrileges, and indifferences by which He Himself is offended. And, through the infinite merits of His most Sacred Heart, and the Immaculate Heart of Mary, I beg of You the conversion of poor sinners.

The Fruits of Fatima

Eucharist Prayer

Most Holy Trinity, I adore Thee! My God, my God, I love Thee in the Most Blessed Sacrament.

Sacrifice Prayer

O Jesus, this is for love of Thee, for the conversion of sinners, and in reparation for offenses committed against the Immaculate Heart of Mary.

About the Author

Joseph Pronechen is a long-time staff writer for EWTN's *National Catholic Register*. His many feature stories have also appeared over the decades in a number of Catholic magazines and newspapers.

Sophia Institute

Sophia Institute is a nonprofit institution that seeks to nurture the spiritual, moral, and cultural life of souls and to spread the Gospel of Christ in conformity with the authentic teachings of the Roman Catholic Church.

Sophia Institute Press fulfills this mission by offering translations, reprints, and new publications that afford readers a rich source of the enduring wisdom of mankind.

Sophia Institute also operates the popular online resource CatholicExchange.com. *Catholic Exchange* provides world news from a Catholic perspective as well as daily devotionals and articles that will help readers to grow in holiness and live a life consistent with the teachings of the Church.

In 2013, Sophia Institute launched Sophia Institute for Teachers to renew and rebuild Catholic culture through service to Catholic education. With the goal of nurturing the spiritual, moral, and cultural life of souls, and an abiding respect for the role and work of teachers, we strive to provide materials and programs that are at once enlightening to the mind and ennobling to the heart; faithful and complete, as well as useful and practical.

Sophia Institute gratefully recognizes the Solidarity Association for preserving and encouraging the growth of our apostolate over the course of many years. Without their generous and timely support, this book would not be in your hands.

www.SophiaInstitute.com
www.CatholicExchange.com
www.SophiaInstituteforTeachers.org